THE WALWORTH FARCE

by Enda Walsh

DINNY	**Denis Conway**
SEAN	**Tadhg Murphy**
BLAKE	**Garrett Lombard**
HAYLEY	**Natalie Best**

DIRECTOR	**Mikel Murfi**
DESIGNER	**Sabine Dargent**
LIGHTING DESIGNER	**Paul Keogan**
CASTING DIRECTOR	**Maureen Hughes**

Production Manager	Eamonn Fox
Company Stage Manager	Sarah Lynch
Assistant Stage Manager	Jen Raith
Technical Manager	Barry O'Brien
Technician	Barry Conway
Costume Supervisor	Doreen McKenna
Carpenter	Gus Dewar
Publicist	Kate Bowe PR

Graphic Design	Bite! Associates
Production Photographer	Keith Pattison

3 – 26 AUGUST 2007
TRAVERSE THEATRE
EDINBURGH

As part of the 2007 Edinburgh Fringe Festival

The Walworth Farce was commissioned by Druid under its new writing programme, DruidNew, and received its première at the Town Hall Theatre, Galway on 20th March 2006 with Denis Conway and Garrett Lombard, with Aaron Monaghan as Sean and Syan Blake as Hayley. The production was also performed at the Everyman Palace Theatre, Cork on 28th March 2006, and the Helix, Dublin on 4th April 2006.

Druid

Druid was founded in Galway in 1975 by three graduates of NUI Galway, Mick Lally, Marie Mullen and Garry Hynes, and its foundation marked the establishment of the first professional theatre company in Ireland outside Dublin. Since then it has been at the forefront of the development of Irish theatre; its regional touring pioneered the Irish touring network and its international success has been unparalleled by any other Irish arts organisation. Recent international touring includes visits to London, Edinburgh, Sydney, Perth, Washington DC, Minneapolis, New York and Tokyo. The company has had two artistic directors: Garry Hynes (1975-91 and 1995 to date) and Maeliosa Stafford (1991-94).

Druid has always worked to reinvigorate perceptions of classic dramatic works and to engage with new dramatic works of a challenging, innovative and daring kind. It has drawn extensively from the Irish dramatic repertoire, including acclaimed productions of classics by Dion Boucicault and M. J. Molloy. Productions that have gone on to gain international recognition include *The Playboy of the Western World* (1982), *At the Black Pig's Dyke* (1992), *Conversations on a Homecoming* (1985), and *Bailegangaire* (1985), featuring Siobhan McKenna in one of her finest dramatic performances. The latter two productions formed part of a major association between Druid and Tom Murphy who was Writer-in-Association with the company and had four of his major works première in Galway.

In 1996 Druid premièred Martin McDonagh's debut work *The Beauty Queen of Leenane*, in a co-production with the Royal Court Theatre. It opened in Galway and subsequently played in London, Sydney, Dublin, and on Broadway, where the production won four Tony Awards, including Best Director for Garry Hynes, the first woman to win the award. In *The Leenane Trilogy* (also with the Royal Court), *The Beauty Queen of Leenane* was joined by premières of McDonagh's *A Skull in Connemara* and *The Lonesome West*. Other recent successes include *My Brilliant Divorce* by Geraldine Aron (a Druid commission that premièred in Galway and was subsequently presented in the West End with Dawn French); and more recently three works by John B. Keane, *Sive* (2002), *Sharon's Grave* (2003) and *The Year of the Hiker* (2006).

DruidSynge, the company's critically acclaimed production of all six of John Millington Synge's plays on the same day, premièred at the Galway Arts Festival in 2005 and has since toured to Minneapolis and Lincoln Center Festival, New York. A production of *The Playboy of the Western World* originating in *DruidSynge* performed at Tokyo International Arts Festival in March 2007.

DruidSynge has been described by Charles Isherwood of The New York Times as *'a highlight not just of my theatregoing year but of my theatregoing life'* and by The Irish Times as *'one of the greatest achievements in the history of Irish theatre.'*

Through its new writing programme, *DruidNew*, Druid has premièred *Leaves* by Lucy Caldwell (2007), *Empress of India* by Stuart Carolan (2006) and *The Walworth Farce* by Enda Walsh (2006); and consistently commissions, develops, and produces new plays by a wide range of emerging and established writers both from Ireland and abroad.

In keeping with its commitment to international classics, following its visit to the Edinburgh Festival Fringe in August 2007 with its production of *The Walworth Farce*, Druid's next production will be Eugene O'Neill's *Long Day's Journey into Night* which will première in Galway on 19 September 2007 before it transfers to the 50th Dublin Theatre Festival.

For more information, including details on forthcoming productions and tours, visit: **www.druidtheatre.com** and **www.druidsynge.com**, and join our mailing list.

'A highlight not just of my theatregoing year but of my theatregoing life' The New York Times on DruidSynge

'Druid has the ability to get under the skin of the new as well as it does the old' Irish Independent

'Druid - taking risks, pushing barriers, discovering new writers' Sunday Tribune

Acknowledgements
Druid is grant aided by the Arts Council of Ireland and gratefully
acknowledges the support of Culture Ireland.

Druid wishes to express its continuing gratitude to Thomas McDonagh
& Company Ltd for their support of the company and gratefully acknowledges
the assistance of Galway City Council and Galway County Council.

Cast

DENIS CONWAY *Dinny*

Druid: *The Walworth Farce* (Galway, Cork and Dublin 2006); *The Playboy of the Western World* (Perth, Australia tour 2005).

Other theatre: *Myrmidons, Making History, Amadeus, Macbeth, Tales from Ovid, Richard III, Mutabilitie, Troilus and Cressida* (for Ouroboros Theatre Co.); *Homeland, A Cry from Heaven, The Dandy Dolls, Riders To The Sea, The Wild Duck, Freedom of the City, The Colleen Bawn, April Bright, The Crucible, The Comedy of Errors* (Abbey & Peacock Theatres); *Diarmuid and Gráinne, Studs, Native City, Buddleia* (for Passion Machine); *Volpone, Castle Rackrent, Miss Julie, The Overcoat, Lear* (for Meridian Theatre Co.).

Film & Television: *Tiger's Tail* (dir John Boorman); *The Wind that Shakes the Barley* (dir Ken Loach); *Boy Eats Girl* (dir Stephen Bradley); *Alexander* (dir Oliver Stone); *Yesterday's Children* (dir Marcus Cole); *Intermission* (dir John Crowley); *The Borstal Boy* (dir Peter Sheridan); *The Countess Cathleen* (dir Paula Bergin); *I Went Down* (dir Paddy Breathnach); *Michael Collins* (dir Neil Jordan); *Making Ends Meet* (dir Declan Recks); *Hide and Seek, Showbands 1 and 2, The Clinic, Bachelors Walk, On Home Ground, Fair City* (RTÉ); *Rebel Heart, Casualty, Custer's Last Stand Up, Ballykissangel* (BBC); *Yesterday's Children* (CBS); *Running Mate, Trí Scéal, Boghaisíní* (TG4).

Denis was awarded The Irish Times/ESB Theatre Award for Best Actor in 2001 for his role as Richard in Ouroboros Theatre Company's production of *Richard III*.

TADHG MURPHY *Sean*

Tadhg trained at the Samuel Beckett Centre, Trinity College Dublin.

Druid: *Empress of India* (Galway and Dublin Theatre Festival 2006).

Other theatre: *Dublin by Lamplight* (for Corn Exchange); *Drive By* (for Performance Corporation); *Taming of the Shrew* (for Rough Magic); *Titus Andronicus* (for Siren Productions); *Shooting Gallery* (for Bedrock Theatre Co.); *Julius Caesar, The Importance of Being Earnest, Harold and Sophie* (Abbey Theatre); *The Goat* (for Landmark Productions); *Deathtrap* (for Red Kettle); *The Real Thing* (for Gúna Nua Theatre Co.); *Fando and Lis,* (Project); *Macbeth, Romeo and Juliet* (for Second Age Theatre Co.); *A Christmas Carol* (Gate Theatre, Dublin); *The Divorcement of Figaro, Triumph of Love, New Morning* (Samuel Beckett Centre); *Oedipus* (Players Theatre, TCD).

Film & Television: *Pride and Joy* (ARC Productions); *Jelly Baby* (Manifesto); *Boy Eats Girl* (Sitric Films); *Alexander* (Intermedial); *Good Man Danny* (DIT); *Hide and Seek* (RTÉ/Accomplice Films); *Love is the Drug* (RTÉ/West Street Films); *No Tears* (One Films).

Radio: numerous plays for RTÉ Radio, including *The Plough and the Stars, The Finnegans* and *The Colleen and the Cowboy.*

Tadhg received a nomination for Best supporting Actor for the feature film *Boy Eats Girl*, at the Irish Film and Television Awards, 2005.

GARRETT LOMBARD *Blake*

Garrett hails from Gorey, Co. Wexford and graduated from
The Samuel Beckett Centre, Trinity College Dublin in 2000.

Druid: *The Year of the Hiker* (Galway, Dublin and National Tour
2006), *The Walworth Farce* (Galway, Cork and Dublin 2006).

Other theatre: *The Cavalcaders* (Abbey Theatre); *Alone It
Stands* (for Lane Productions); *Playing from the Heart* (The Ark);
The Field (national tour of Scott-Rellis Productions); *Our Country's
Good, 'Tis Pity She's A Whore, Artists and Admirers, Attempts
On Her Life* (for TCD's Acting Studies).

Film & Television: *Rough Diamond* (RTÉ); *Love is the Drug*
(Saffron Pictures/RTÉ); *Pure Mule* (Accomplice Television/RTÉ –
for which Garrett received an IFTA nomination); *Alexander*
(dir Oliver Stone); *Frontline* (dir David Gleeson); *Fair City* (RTÉ).

NATALIE BEST *Hayley*

Druid: *The Walworth Farce* marks Natalie's debut with Druid.

Other theatre: *Icarus Girl* (Arcola); *The Alchemist, Life of Galileo*
(Royal National Theatre); *Aladdin and the Enchanted Lamp* (Bristol
Old Vic); *Women Laughing, Semi-Monde* (Mountview Academy);
Ubu Roi, Oh What a Lovely War (Brentwood Theatre and Horizon).

Film & Television: *Honest* (ITV/Greenlight); *Daphne, Holby City*
(BBC).

Creative Team

ENDA WALSH *Writer*

Druid: *The Walworth Farce* is Enda's first play with Druid.

Theatre: *How Much is Your Iron?* (translated from Bertolt Brecht's original, Young Vic, March 2007); *Chatroom* (Cottesloe, Royal National Theatre, March 2006, Autumn 2007); *The New Electric Ballroom* (Kammerspeil Theatre Munich, winner of Theater Heute's Best Foreign Play 2005); *The Small Things* (for Paines Plough, Menier Chocolate Factory, London and Galway Arts Festival 2005); two short plays, *How These Men Talk* (Zurich Shauspielehaus) and *Lyndie's Gotta Gun for Artistas Unidos* (Lisbon's National Theatre); *Bedbound* (Dublin Theatre Festival 2000, Edinburgh 2001 – Fringe First Winner, Royal Court, London, New York and worldwide); *Misterman* (Granary Theatre); *Disco Pigs* (Cork, Dublin, 1996; Edinburgh, 1997; West End 1998, Stewart Parker and George Devine Awards 1997); *The Ginger Ale Boy* (Corcadorca). In development, an adaptation of Dostoevsky's *The Brothers Karamazov* for Theatre O.

Film: *Disco Pigs* (Temple Films/Renaissance). In development, Hunger (Blast/FILMFOUR/Channel 4, shooting September 2007); *Island of the Aunts* (an adaptation of Eva Ibbotson's children's novel for Cuba Pictures); *Chatroom* (for Ruby Films/FILMFOUR and Scott Rudin Films); *Kinderboy* (Blast/Channel 4).

Radio: *Four Big Days in the Life of Dessie Banks* (RTÉ Radio – winner of the PPI Award for Best Radio Drama 2001); *The Monotonous Life of Little Miss P* (BBC – commended in the Berlin Prix Europa 2003).

Enda is currently Writer-in-Association with the Abbey Theatre, Dublin.

MIKEL MURFI *Director*

Mikel trained at Ecole Jacques Lecoq, Paris.

Druid: As an actor, *The Increased Difficulty Of Concentration*.

Other theatre: As an actor, *The Chairs* (Blue Raincoat); *The Cure* (The Half Moon Theatre, Cork); *The Morning After Optimism, The Playboy of The Western World, The Tempest,*

The Comedy of Errors (Abbey and Peacock Theatres); *Strokehauling, SickDyingDeadBuriedOut, Half Eight Mass of a Tuesday, Come Down from the Mountain John Clown, John Clown, Macbeth* (Barabbas), *God's Gift* (& national tour), *The White Headed Boy* (& national and US tours); *Studs, Melting Penguins* (Passion Machine); *Lady Windemere's Fan* (Rough Magic); *The Tender Trap* (Pigsback).

As a director, *Diamonds in the Soil, The Lost Days of Ollie Deasy* (for Macnas); *The Mysteries* (as co-director, Macnas); *Trad* (Galway Arts Festival Production); *The Lonesome West* (Lyric Theatre, Belfast).

Film & Television: As an actor, *Ella Enchanted, The Last September, Sweety Barrett, The Butcher Boy, Love and Rage, Guiltrip, Words Upon The Window Pane, The Three Joes, The Commitments.*

As a director, *Druma* (a short film for Macnas); *John Duffy's Brother* (for Parkfilms based on the Flann O'Brien short story).

Awards: Best Irish Production, Dublin Theatre Festival for *The Lost Days of Ollie Deasy*; Fringe First, Edinburgh 2005 for *Trad*.

Mikel is presently working on a theatre show that takes place entirely underwater.

SABINE DARGENT *Set and Costume Designer*

Sabine is a French designer living in Ireland.

Druid: *The Walworth Farce* is Sabine's first design with Druid (nominated for an Irish Times Theatre Award 2006).

Other theatre: *Henry and Harriet* (various shops, Belfast); *To Have and to Hold* (Old Museum Belfast); *Days of Wine and Roses* (Lyric Theatre, Belfast); *Dublin Carol* (Everyman Palace, Cork); *The Bacchae of Baghdad, The Importance of Being Earnest* (Abbey Theatre); *Antigone, Hard to Believe* (Storytellers Theatre Co.); *Ghosts* (ESB/Irish Times Best Set Design Award in 2003), *The Lonesome West* (Lyric Theatre, Belfast); *Monged, Pilgrims in the Park, Tadhg Stray Wandered In* (Fishamble); *How Many Miles to Babylon?* (Second Age); *The Shadow of the Glen, The Tinker's Wedding* (Big Telly); *Martha, Little Rudolf* (Barnstorm); *Jack Fell Down, Burning Dreams, Last Call* (Team); *The Tempest* (Blue Raincoat); *Desert Lullaby* (Galloglass); *Hysteria* (B*spoke).

She designed and performed painting in *Senses* (Rex Levitates).

France: In France she designed for TGV and was in-house design assistant to Serge Noyelle (Théâtre de Chatillon) and Antonio Diaz Florian (l'Epée de Bois). She was assistant to Lucio Fanti on En attendant Godot directed by Bernard Sobel (Théâtre de Gennevilliers). Sabine has been working mostly in theatre, but also on film and exhibitions.

PAUL KEOGAN *Lighting Designer*

Born in Dublin, Paul studied Drama at The Samuel Beckett Centre, Trinity College Dublin, and at Glasgow University. After graduating he worked as Production Manager for Project Arts Centre.

Druid: *The Walworth Farce; The Spirit of Annie Ross.*

Other theatre: *Julius Caesar, The Electrocution of Children, Amazing Grace, Living Quarters, Making History, The Map Maker's Sorrow, Cúirt an Mheán Oíche, Mrs. Warren's Profession, Bailegangaire, Down the Line, Eden, The Wild Duck, The Tempest, Melonfarmer, Portia Coughlan, Homeland* (also set design), *Heavenly Bodies* (Abbey and Peacock Theatres); *Performances, Gates of Gold, Festen* (Gate Theatre, Dublin); *La Musica, Titus Andronicus* (Siren Productions); *Pierrot Lunaire* (Almeida Opera); *Trad* (also set design, Galway Arts Festival); *Tintype, The Old Tune/Night* (also set design, Kilkenny Arts Festival); *Harvest* (Royal Court Theatre, London); *Blue/Orange* (Crucible Theatre, Sheffield, and UK Tour); *The Makropulos Case, Un Ballo in Maschera, Der Fliegende Holländer* (Opera Zuid, Netherlands); *The Queen of Spades, L'Elisir d'Amore, Lady Macbeth of Mtensk, The Silver Tassie* (Opera Ireland); *The Lighthouse* (Opera Theatre Company); *Maria di Rohan, Pénlope, Susannah, Don Gregorio, Transformations, Rusalka, The Silver Lake* (Wexford Festival Opera); *Woyzeck* (also set design, Corcadorca).

Paul also designed The Wishing Well, a large-scale outdoor projection piece for Kilkenny Arts Festival 1999, and the lighting for the Irish Pavilion at the Architectural Biennale in Venice 2004 and 2006.

Paul is an associate artist of the Abbey Theatre, Dublin and was the recipient of the Gerard Arnhold Bursary at Wexford Festival Opera 2006.

THE WALWORTH FARCE

Enda Walsh

To the first director of this play
Mikel Murfi
for his advice, support, enthusiasm and general brilliance.
Thank you so much.

Characters
in order of appearance

DINNY, *fifty, Irish accent*
BLAKE, *twenty-five, Irish accent*
SEAN, *twenty-four, Irish accent*
HAYLEY, *twenty-four, South London accent*

This text went to press before the end of rehearsals and may differ slightly from the play as performed.

ACT ONE

The set is three square spaces. Essentially a living room at its centre, a kitchen to stage left and a bedroom to stage right.

Much of the plasterboard has been removed from the walls and what remains are the wooden frames beneath.

The two doors on the wall leading into the kitchen and the two doors leading into the bedroom on the other wall have been removed.

The back wall shows the front door leading into this flat.

There are two wardrobes at the back made from the plaster-board. One on the left and one on the right of the front door.

The decor is at best drab. Everything worn and colourless and stuck in the 1970s.

There is an armchair and a small coffee table in the sitting room with six cans of Harp on it. The kitchen is fitted and very messy. The bedroom has two single beds on top of each other made to look like bunk beds.

We're in a council flat on the Walworth Road, South London.

As the lights go up we see a man sitting in the armchair. This is the father, DINNY. *He wears a bad brown yellowing wig on his head, a tight ill-fitting suit that makes him look clownish. He has a jet black bushy moustache. He's holding a small biscuit tin.*

On a side table next to him he presses the button of an old tape recorder. 'An Irish Lullaby' begins to play. Slowly he opens the biscuit tin. He looks inside, smiles and smells the contents. He closes it and places it under the armchair. He begins to polish his shoes with a tin of brown polish.

His son BLAKE *stands in his vest and underpants and irons something on a coffin-shaped cardboard box in the bedroom.*

BLAKE*'s brother* SEAN *stands in the kitchen. He wears a woollen hat. He takes it off and places it in the pocket of his jacket. His hair has been shaved so that he looks as if he's badly balding.*

He goes to the table where he looks into a Tesco bag. His expression suddenly shocked. He takes out an extremely large salami sausage. He goes to the oven and flings the sausage inside, closing the door. With trepidation he returns to the Tesco bag, reaches in and takes out a packet of Ryvita crackers. Again he's shook.

DINNY *enters the kitchen carrying the tape recorder and* SEAN *quickly hides the Ryvita behind his back.* DINNY *pours himself a glass of water and gargles for a bit.* SEAN *watches him.* DINNY *spits it back in the sink, turns and exits the kitchen and back into the sitting room.*

DINNY *places the tape recorder on the side table and starts to do little physical jerks. He's exercising.*

BLAKE *is putting on what he was ironing. A floral skirt. He puts the iron under the bed and takes up a freshly ironed colourful blouse. He smells it. It's not the best. He sprays it with some Mister Sheen. He smells it again and puts it on. From under the bed he takes an old lamp with an orange floral shade. He slings it off a hook that hangs from the ceiling and turns it on. The bedroom is thrown into a new light.*

SEAN *meanwhile is making Ryvita sandwiches in the kitchen with spreadable cheese he's taken from a tiny fridge.*

DINNY *stops exercising. He takes off his wig and we can see some Velcro tape running on top of his head which obviously keeps on the wig. He takes a comb out and gives the wig a quick once over.*

BLAKE *puts on a woman's black permed wig. He picks up the cardboard coffin and exits the bedroom and into the sitting room and stands waiting.*

SEAN *sticks a bad fake moustache on (à la Magnum P.I.), dons a tight cream sports jacket which he buttons up and exits the kitchen.* BLAKE *hands him the coffin and enters one of the wardrobes.*

6

SEAN *stands holding the coffin on his shoulders by the front door and waits for his father.*

DINNY *sticks his wig back on. He goes to the wall and takes a small golden trophy off a shelf. He reverentially kisses it before carefully replacing it. He blesses himself.*

He takes a deep breath and exhales sharply. He's ready.

DINNY *holds the other end of the coffin with* SEAN. *He reaches to the light switch on the back wall and switches off the light in the sitting room as 'An Irish Lullaby' comes to an end.*

The room is thrown into darkness and silence. DINNY *immediately turns the light back on.*

DINNY. She was our mother, Paddy –

> *Suddenly the tape recorder blasts out the Irish traditional song 'A Nation Once Again'.*

> *The two of them startled.*

Shite!

> DINNY *turns off the tape recorder. Again he takes a deep breath and exhales sharply. He then reaches back to the light switch and turns the lights off again. He immediately turns them back on.*

> *The Farce begins. The three speak in Cork City accents. The performance style resembles The Three Stooges.*

She was our mother, Paddy, and she treated us well.

SEAN AS PADDY. It was a happy outcome, Dinny, even if it was her funeral.

DINNY. To see her little smiling face all done up in that make-up, looking like a movie star, wasn't she?

SEAN AS PADDY. A little miracle how her head was recreated when you think of the wallop that horse gave her. Hit by a dead horse. Who would have believed it?

DINNY. As the priest said, Paddy . . . only the good Lord knows of our final curtain.

7

SEAN AS PADDY. I fear He does.

DINNY. It was God's will to send a massive dead stallion careering over a hedge.

SEAN AS PADDY. Yes.

DINNY. God's will to send it crashing on top our sweet mother's tiny body as she innocently picked gooseberries for her own consumption on that quiet country road. Whatever way you look at it, Paddy, religion's awful cruel.

SEAN AS PADDY. Is that cans of beer over there?

DINNY. It is, they are.

SEAN AS PADDY. It's just she's getting awful heavy . . .

DINNY. Stick her in the dining room there, Paddy. Don't want my two little boys having nightmares.

SEAN *and* DINNY *take the coffin into the bedroom.*

SEAN AS PADDY. So this is your place, Dinny?

DINNY. Built with my own hands . . . figuratively speaking of course. Not much call for building work in my line of work.

BLAKE AS MAUREEN *enters from the wardrobe.*

BLAKE AS MAUREEN. You want me to fix the sandwiches, Dinny?

DINNY. Go heavy on the cheese spread, sweetheart. You know how I like my sandwiches, Maureen love.

BLAKE AS MAUREEN. Where's the kitchen?

DINNY *secretly and aggressively points over to where it is.*

BLAKE AS MAUREEN *quickly enters the kitchen. He immediately takes off his wig and puts on a new red-haired permed wig and re-enters the wardrobe.*

SEAN AS PADDY. What is it you do again, Dinny?

DINNY. Brain surgery, Paddy.

SEAN AS PADDY. And to think you were thrown out of school at fifteen.

DINNY. Ireland's a terrible hole and you'll get no argument from me . . . but I'll say this about it . . . it gives fools a fighting chance.

SEAN AS PADDY. Fair play.

DINNY. Not like London, Paddy?

SEAN AS PADDY. London's a tough old nut. For a while I was working the sites but London's all grown up now and not much building for fellas like me. Truth is I haven't worked for six years, Dinny.

DINNY. You've flat feet of course.

SEAN AS PADDY. The flat feet are only half of it, there's more. Being a man of medicine you may have heard of my condition.

DINNY. You've got a condition?

SEAN AS PADDY. A critical condition.

DINNY. Proceed.

SEAN AS PADDY. I'm getting pains in my hole, Dinny.

DINNY (*carefully*). Yes.

SEAN AS PADDY. Remember as a little boy that big railing I impaled myself on . . . pierced my back?

DINNY. Oh that hole!

SEAN AS PADDY. It just missed the heart, didn't it. When I get too excited, Dinny, I fall over . . .

DINNY. Do ya?

SEAN AS PADDY. I do! Blood stops racing to the head . . . I collapse.

DINNY. Collapse!? Good Lord!

SEAN AS PADDY. Doctor says one day I might never wake up. Thought it might happen to me today what with Mammy and everything.

DINNY. You had a pain in your hole today?

SEAN AS PADDY. A shocking pain in my hole, Dinny.

DINNY. Well, you listen to me, little brother. I wasn't always there for you in the past.

SEAN AS PADDY. You were never there for me.

DINNY. That's right, you're right. But in the future. If there's anything you want, if that hole of yours is keeping you awake at night just pick up the telephone and give us a call.

Enter BLAKE AS VERA *from the wardrobe.*

BLAKE AS VERA. Those two boys of yours are terrorising a copper outside.

DINNY. The little feckers. Sort that out for us, Paddy.

SEAN AS PADDY *runs and disappears into the wardrobe closing the door behind him.*

BLAKE AS VERA. Well, haven't you done well for yourself!? Beautiful leather couch, lovely little ornaments. Nice shag carpet. That seen any action has it?

DINNY. Now a gentleman wouldn't say, Vera.

BLAKE AS VERA. He wouldn't but you would.

DINNY *and* BLAKE AS VERA *laugh.*

DINNY (*laughing*). Oh very good, very good!

BLAKE AS VERA. How'd you make the big leap from painting and decorating to brain surgery?

DINNY. Oh you might well ask that question, Vera love.

BLAKE AS VERA. I just did, Denis.

A pause.

DINNY. One day . . .

BLAKE AS VERA. Yes?

DINNY *really has to think hard about this.*

DINNY. . . . a few years ago . . . I was busy applying some paint to a client's wall. Now she was a woman who was forever complaining about headaches and such like.

'Denis,' she would say, 'I have such a terrible pounding in the head.' Well, the poor dear fell in front of me and cracked her head wide open. And there I was looking at my first brain. (*Easier now.*) Now I liken the brain to a walnut, Vera. Larger obviously and not the class of thing you'd hand out to kiddies at Hallowe'en . . . but a walnut all the same. She was still breathing so I had to act fast. Now Coca-Cola, which I had on my person for its thirst-quenching properties, is also a terrific . . . terrific preservative. Her head took two litres of Coca-Cola and a roll of masking tape to bind her right back up. The doctors said I saved her life because of my quick thinking, suggested to me a night course in basic brain surgery as I obviously had the knack for it and two years later . . . here I am!

BLAKE AS VERA (*she's not convinced*). That's quite a story.

DINNY. It certainly is.

SEAN *re-enters from the wardrobe as his seven-year-old self.*

SEAN. All right we play in the back garden, Dad?

DINNY. Yes, Sean. Where's Blake?

BLAKE. Here, Dad.

DINNY. I want you to stay out there for the afternoon and look after your little brother, all right, Blake?!

BLAKE (*in awe*). This place is beautiful.

DINNY (*growling*). Outside outside!

BLAKE *and* SEAN *run and enter a wardrobe.*

DINNY *looks very agitated.*

BLAKE AS VERA *and* SEAN AS PADDY *re-enter.*

SEAN AS PADDY. The little devils.

DINNY. Copper, all right?

SEAN AS PADDY. He was crying a little bit.

DINNY. They're feisty boys, them! Take after their old man.

SEAN AS PADDY. Little tearaways you mean.

DINNY. Tearaways! Not at all.

BLAKE AS VERA. The way they acted in mass.

DINNY. Giddy that's all.

BLAKE AS VERA. They set fire to a nun, Dinny.

DINNY. In fairness, they didn't know it was a nun. She frightened the life out of them, that's all.

BLAKE AS VERA. She was in a terrible state.

DINNY. Arrah she was put out wasn't she . . . eventually.

SEAN AS PADDY. You shouldn't have given them those Mars Bars earlier.

BLAKE AS VERA. Church is no place for Mars Bars, Dinny.

BLAKE *enters the kitchen and changes into* MAUREEN*'s wig*.

DINNY. No place is no place for Mars Bars, Vera. The fact is the Mars Bar's like eating shit on a stick. Worse . . . sure doesn't it rot your teeth.

BLAKE AS MAUREEN *re-enters with Ryvita sandwiches on a plate*.

(*Announcing*.) Ahh sandwiches, great stuff, Maureen! My favourites aren't they?

SEAN *looks very nervous*.

BLAKE AS MAUREEN. Spreadable cheddar, Dinny . . .

DINNY *freezes when he sees them*.

DINNY. What's this?

BLAKE (*as himself*). Sandwiches, Dad.

DINNY. Ryvita sandwiches?

SEAN. There was no sliced pan in Tesco, Dad.

DINNY. Supermarket, isn't it?

SEAN. I know but . . .

12

DINNY. Didn't you go?

SEAN. I did, Dad.

DINNY. You didn't go.

SEAN. I did.

DINNY. Don't answer me back or I'll thump ya!

BLAKE. Maybe we –

DINNY. Shut up, you! The story calls for sliced pan bread, doesn't it?

SEAN. I know but –

DINNY. The story doesn't work if we don't have the facts and Ryvitas aren't the facts . . . they're not close to the facts. A batched loaf is close to the facts, a bread roll is closer still but a Ryvita? . . . A Ryvita's just taking the piss, Sean. A Ryvita's a great leap of the imagination.

BLAKE. It's the right cheese.

DINNY. Feck the cheese! It's sticking out like a sore thumb. Your mother would never make crispy sandwiches, would she? You two little boys playing out in the garden out there . . . you'll not be happy with Ryvita!

SEAN. I can go back to Tesco if you want.

DINNY. Ah forget about it. And another thing, don't be cutting corners, you!

SEAN. How'd you mean?

DINNY. 'London's a tough old nut. For a while I was working the sites but London's all grown up now and not much building for fellas like me.' Then what, then what?

SEAN. Truth is I haven't worked for six years . . .

DINNY. 'The truth be told the Irishman is not the master builder of yesteryear. That title belongs to the men of Eastern Europe. Built like buses they are. Feet like double beds. The truth is I haven't worked for six years, Dinny.'

SEAN. That's a new line, Dad.

DINNY. So?

SEAN. You want me to use it?

DINNY. Getting lazy on me?

SEAN. No, Dad.

DINNY. Sloppy, Sean.

SEAN. Sorry, Dad.

DINNY. You wanna get your act together. There'll be no chance of the actin' trophy gathering dust on your shelf if you don't pull up them socks, boy.

SEAN. Right, Dad.

DINNY (*pointing to the trophy*). The acting trophy, Sean!

SEAN. Yes, Dad.

DINNY. Acting trophy!

SEAN. I know, Dad.

DINNY. Blake, make your entrance.

    BLAKE *turns back into the kitchen. He sighs.*

BLAKE (*to himself*). Shite.

DINNY (*to SEAN*). We'll talk about this later, right?!

SEAN. All right, Dad.

    BLAKE AS MAUREEN *re-enters with the sandwiches.*

DINNY. Ahh sandwiches, great stuff! My favourites aren't they, Maureen?

BLAKE AS MAUREEN. Spreadable cheddar, Dinny.

DINNY. Ohh lovely! Rich and creamy.

    He bites into the Ryvita sandwich but it crumbles all over the place. He grimaces and looks like he's about to explode but SEAN quickly continues the performance.

SEAN AS PADDY. Terrible shock going all the way to the cemetery and not being able to stick Mammy in the ground.

DINNY. A disgrace.

SEAN AS PADDY. Whoever heard of a gravedigger without a digger. Like a postman without post, a brickie without bricks, a shopkeeper without a shop, a cook without a cooker, a footballer without a foot, a bus driver without a bus, a fishmonger without a fish –

BLAKE AS VERA (*stopping him*). Paddy!

SEAN AS PADDY. Awful though. You had every right to hit that gravedigger as we left for home, Dinny.

DINNY. Couldn't get up much speed in that hearse though.

SEAN AS PADDY. No.

DINNY. Still . . . I managed to reverse and have another pop off the little fecker. (*Laughs a little.*)

SEAN AS PADDY. Christ it's great to be back with the big brother! The brain surgeon living in the gaff on the hill overlooking Cork City in all its finery.

DINNY. And what news of London Town, Paddy? This Walworth Road off the Elephant and Castle, paint me a picture of this boulevard and its surrounding environs.

SEAN AS PADDY *clears his throat.*

SEAN AS PADDY. On my palate is only grey, Dinny.

DINNY. Right.

SEAN AS PADDY. Grey and muck. For these are the two primary colours that make up much of the Elephant.

DINNY. I see.

SEAN AS PADDY. And as for the Castle . . . not so much a fortress, for a billion cars daily circle this grassy knoll known as 'the roundabout'.

DINNY. 'Daily traverse'!

SEAN AS PADDY. For a billion cars daily *traverse* this grassy knoll known as 'the roundabout'.

DINNY. Better.

SEAN AS PADDY. A million tiny bedsits there are. Large carbuncles sprouting out from the ground. Massive flats. Deadly, pitiful places that even the rats have abandoned, the cockroaches have done cockroaching and all that's left is London people.

DINNY. Jaynee.

SEAN AS PADDY. To sum it up in pure Cork parlance . . . the place is a hole.

BLAKE AS VERA. The lot of London is, Dinny.

DINNY. You do often read stories that they do eat their young over there, Paddy and Vera. So criminal and violent they are that Londoners like nothing more than skinning an Irishman halfway through his drink.

SEAN AS PADDY. Sacrilegious, boy. Sacrilegious. (*He knocks back his can of beer.*)

BLAKE AS VERA. And what news of Cork City, Dinny?

DINNY. Well, Vera, my love, there she is laid out in front of us.

SEAN AS PADDY. Aw beautiful.

DINNY. Laid out in all her finery.

BLAKE AS VERA (*wistfully*). Ah Cork.

DINNY. I often do stand here after a long day brain-surgeoning and just drink in this wonderful sight with a fine glass of red wine and a packet of those green Pringles. For I liken Cork City to a large jewel, Paddy and Vera.

SEAN AS PADDY. Do ya?

DINNY. I do. A jewel with the majestic River Lee ambling through it, chopping the diamond in two before making its way to murkier climes . . . towards the poisonous Irish Sea for example. Ah yes, Cork City. You could call it Ireland's jewel but you'd be A FUCKING IDIOT, BOY. FOR IT IS, REALLY AND TRULY, IRELAND'S TRUE CAPITAL CITY.

SEAN *and* BLAKE *applaud.*

SEAN AS PADDY. Oh well said, Dinny!

DINNY. The red and the white, Paddy! The blood and the bandage, little brother! Blood and the bandage!

BLAKE AS VERA. I'll help Maureen prepare the chicken.

BLAKE AS VERA *goes to the kitchen and opens the oven. He nearly falls back in horror. He slams it shut immediately.*

SEAN AS PADDY. And Dinny, tell me, tell me . . . would Mammy stand beside you and look at this very same view?

DINNY. She would, Paddy. She would. Me with my red wine, her standing with a pint of Beamish in her hand.

SEAN AS PADDY (*smiling*). Ah yes.

DINNY. A bottle of Harp in her other hand.

SEAN AS PADDY. That's right.

DINNY. A large glass of whiskey by the coffee table.

SEAN AS PADDY. That's her.

DINNY. And a can of Heineken in her coat pocket.

SEAN AS PADDY. She loved her drink.

DINNY (*with admiration*). You know when they pulled that horse off her, you could actually smell the whiskey from her blood. I mean, that's incredible, boy.

SEAN AS PADDY. And I always thought it would be the drink that would finally kill her.

DINNY. Well, it was in a way, Paddy. Those gooseberries she was gathering were for fermenting in a lethal vat of alcohol she called her 'Preservative'.

SEAN AS PADDY. Ohh the irony.

DINNY. I know, cruel, isn't it? (*Instructing him.*) 'So what about the will, Dinny?!'

SEAN AS PADDY. So what about the will, Dinny?

DINNY (*snaps*). Jesus, Sean, quicker! Quicker!

SEAN AS PADDY. Did she mention to you what might be in the will?

DINNY *takes a moment, furious that* SEAN *has messed up. The two boys tense. Suddenly:*

DINNY. The will, she did, Paddy! She gave me a hint a few weeks ago. But as custom will have it, the will must be read with the wives present.

SEAN AS PADDY (*eagerly calling*). Vera, love, the will!

DINNY (*just as eager and rubbing his hands*). Maureen, sweetheart, the reading of the will.

BLAKE *comes running from the kitchen wearing* MAUREEN*'s wig and carrying* VERA*'s wig.*

The three enter the bedroom and surround the coffin.

Read it loud and clear, Maureen.

BLAKE *takes the will from a sealed envelope and reads it.*

BLAKE AS MAUREEN. 'To my loving sons Denis and Patrick.'

SEAN AS PADDY. Nice touch.

BLAKE AS MAUREEN. 'I'm on the bus back home from the pub and fairly tanked up so here's the will. As your father would say, you two boys were the only family we ever had, you weren't much but we loved you . . . though we never got around to showing it on account of the terrible poverty we were under.'

DINNY. That's true.

BLAKE AS MAUREEN. 'But as you know the house you grew up in is now worth a few bob and can be carved up between the both of you.

DINNY *clears his throat.*

However, it's my wish that the son who is the most sensible, the most successful with his own money, the most balanced in his own life, should act as executor of the estate.

DINNY *has started to smile and nod to himself.*

That son will organise a small allowance to be paid monthly into his brother's account so that he doesn't piss it up a wall.

DINNY *fails to suppress his laughter.*

(*Quickly.*) A memorandum of the special gifts I want divided between family members is listed below. All the best in life. The bus is stopped so that's me off to the chipper. Mammy.'

DINNY (*erupting*). Well, that's clear as clear!

SEAN AS PADDY. How d'you mean?

DINNY. Take a look around you, Paddy. A far cry from Walworth Road and its deserting rats, aren't we?

SEAN AS PADDY. Suppose.

DINNY. She had mentioned to me she was worried the money wouldn't be handled sensibly what with our histories. She's looking for a steady hand, you see.

BLAKE AS VERA. He's lying, he's lying, Paddy!

SEAN AS PADDY (*looking at the will*). He's not, Vera! That's Mammy's will all right. You can smell the Bushmills off it.

DINNY. Fear not, little brother. As controller of the estate and your yearly allowance I'll make sure things are completely transparent.

SEAN AS PADDY. Monthly allowance.

DINNY. In the meantime we can keep ourselves happy with the personal gifts left in the memorandum by Mammy. Maureen, sweetheart.

BLAKE AS MAUREEN (*reading*). 'My deep fat fryer for my son Denis.'

DINNY (*triumphantly*). Yes!

BLAKE AS MAUREEN. 'And three cans of Harp for Patrick.'

SEAN AS PADDY. Ah Jesus.

DINNY (*laughing*). Three cans of Harp! You always were her favourite. You need a hand basting that chicken, Maureen!?

DINNY *and* BLAKE AS MAUREEN *leave the bedroom and walk across to the kitchen.*

(*Still laughing.*) Jesus but it's working like a dream.

BLAKE AS MAUREEN (*distracted*). This house is beautiful.

DINNY (*laughing*). A brain surgeon!? Can you believe it?! We'll fill them with the roast chicken and get them on the car ferry back to London. A monthly allowance? He's got two chances . . . none and . . .

BLAKE *pulls a baking tray out of the oven with the huge salami sausage on it. Seeing it:*

(*Snaps and screams.*) SEAN!

SEAN. Coming, Dad!

SEAN *comes running from the bedroom towards the kitchen.* DINNY *grabs a large frying pan.*

DINNY (*growls to himself*). A fecking sausage!?

SEAN *enters and immediately* DINNY *swings the frying pan across the back of* SEAN*'s head.* SEAN *hits the floor fast.*

A long pause as DINNY *and* BLAKE *look at* SEAN *on the floor.*

DINNY *takes a cup of water and gargles a little. He then spits it out on* SEAN*'s head.*

(*To* BLAKE, *calmly.*) Get him up and sort him out.

DINNY *goes back into the living room and sits in the armchair. He takes his wig off. He takes up a massive bottle of moisturising cream, squeezes some in his hand and aggressively applies it to his face and head.*

BLAKE *helps* SEAN *up.*

SEAN *sits at the table and* BLAKE *stands.*

A long pause.

The two brothers talk in hushed tones.

BLAKE. Are you okay?

SEAN. Yeah.

A pause.

BLAKE. What's with the shopping?

SEAN. I picked up the wrong bag in Tesco. (*A pause.*) It was a mistake.

BLAKE *looks in at* DINNY.

What's he doing?

BLAKE. Puttin' on his cream.

BLAKE *faces into the kitchen.*

A long pause.

SEAN. Something else happened to me, Blake.

BLAKE. Did someone try to get ya?

SEAN. No. No one ever does. You should come out with me the next time.

BLAKE *doesn't respond.*

A pause.

DINNY *is smelling the contents of the biscuit tin again.*

BLAKE. When we came here as little kids you could still smell Ireland from our jumpers.

SEAN (*distantly*). Yeah.

BLAKE. You could smell Mammy's cooking, couldn't you? It was roast chicken that last day and it was a lovely smell, hey Sean? And I think we might have come across on a boat . . . (*Prompting* SEAN, *smiling.*) Go on.

BLAKE *holds* SEAN*'s hand.*

SEAN (*continuing*). And despite the sea and wind, the smell of Mammy's cooking and that chicken was still stuck in the wool of our jumpers.

BLAKE. And I can't remember getting off a boat . . . but maybe we got a bus then to London, Sean, and still Mammy right around us.

SEAN. And Dad must have locked the door as soon as we were inside because the smell sort of stayed longer.

BLAKE. And for a while it stayed and we must have talked about the chicken smell and we must have missed Mammy, hey Sean?

SEAN. Yeah, we must have.

BLAKE. Dad all talk of Ireland, Sean. Everything's Ireland. His voice is stuck in Cork so it's impossible to forget what Cork is. (*A pause.*) This story we play is everything. (*A pause.*) Once upon a time my head was full of pictures of Granny's coffin and Mr and Mrs Cotter and Paddy and Vera and Bouncer the dog and all those busy pictures in our last day. (*Smiling.*) 'Cause you'd say Dad's words and they'd give you pictures, wouldn't they, Sean? And so many pictures in your head . . . Sure you wouldn't want for the outside world even if it was a good world! You could be happy. (*A pause.*) But all them pictures have stopped. I say his words and all I can see is the word. A lot of words piled on top of other words. There's no sense to my day 'cause the sense isn't important anymore. No pictures. No dreams. Words only. (*A pause.*) All I've got is the memory of the roast chicken, Sean.

DINNY *enters the kitchen.*

DINNY. Explain the shopping to me then?

SEAN. A mistake, Dad.

DINNY. How a mistake?

SEAN. Someone tricked me with the wrong bag.

DINNY. Did they?

SEAN. Yes, Dad.

DINNY. Who?

SEAN. The girl at the cash register.

DINNY. Made fun of you, did she? Tricked you and then had a good laugh?

SEAN. She was a little bitch, Dad.

DINNY. She was a little bitch. And many more feckers out there, Sean, wanting to gobble you up.

SEAN. I can go back if you want.

DINNY. You're not enjoying going outside are you?

SEAN. Only if you want me to.

DINNY. Seems to me you might be enjoying it a little.

SEAN. No.

DINNY. Not like Blake here who knows he can't go out.

SEAN. I hate it too, Dad.

DINNY. Do you?

SEAN. I do.

DINNY. Are you lying to me about this girl that tricked you?

SEAN. No, Dad.

DINNY. 'Cause if you lie to me there'll be terrible trouble to pay.

SEAN. I know there will. There's no lying going on.

DINNY. Blake?

BLAKE. Yes, Dad.

DINNY. You're awful quiet.

BLAKE. Just keeping my energy. I know it's about to get real fast soon so just thinking things through again, that's all.

DINNY. Got your eyes on the actin' trophy, Blake? Such a prize.

BLAKE. Sure it's only you that gets to win it.

DINNY. But feck it, you're almost there, boy, almost.

BLAKE. Am I, Dad?

DINNY. You are. You've got the tough job playing the ladies, of course. (*Slight pause*.) Sort of nice playing Mammy though?

BLAKE. Yes, Dad.

DINNY. Christ she's a great woman, all right! A great woman! She'll be waiting in the kitchen back in Cork, lads! Waiting for her three men to walk back through the door.

BLAKE. When might that be, Dad? (*Slight pause*.) When?

DINNY *slowly inhales and announces loudly,*

DINNY. One day . . . ! One day!!

SEAN *races to the wardrobe.*

One day I'll buy a house just like this one, Maureen!

BLAKE *throws the sausage back in the oven and runs over and joins* SEAN *in the wardrobe.*

One day, by Jesus the Holy Christ, I'll live in a castle overlooking the banks of the lovely Lee. One day, mark my words! One day!

Large thumping noise and DINNY *is startled.*

By jaynee, who's this at the door?

SEAN *and* BLAKE *enter as Mr Cotter,* JACK, *and his brother-in-law* PETER *(both from Montenotte). They are carrying another cardboard coffin on their shoulders.*

BLAKE AS JACK. Watch the paintwork, Peter.

SEAN AS PETER. Sorry, Jack.

DINNY *freezes in the kitchen as he hears them.*

BLAKE AS JACK. I've just got a man in to do it for me actually. But by Jesus, what a day!

A gravedigger without a digger!? Have you ever heard of such shite.

SEAN AS PETER. Like a banker without a bank, a journalist without a journal, a painter without paint, a producer without produce, a publican without a pub, a zookeeper without a zoo . . .

BLAKE AS JACK. The list can go on, Peter, and we can just stand here with your dead father stuck in this box breaking my delicate little shoulders.

SEAN AS PETER. Well, it's your house, Jack, where do you want him?

BLAKE AS JACK. Stick him in the kitchen and out of my sight.

As they go into the kitchen, DINNY *runs out and across into the bedroom.*

BLAKE *and* SEAN *place the coffin down on the kitchen table.*

DINNY (*to himself*). By jaynee I wasn't expecting this at all! (*To* PADDY.) Back inside! Back inside! Look I'm sorry, Paddy, but they just called out of the blue. It wouldn't be appropriate to . . .

DINNY *has to wait for the two boys and is annoyed by this.*

(*Snapping.*) Move it, lads, for fuck sakes!

SEAN *exits the kitchen and runs over to the bedroom.* BLAKE *runs back to the wardrobe and enters it.*

SEAN AS PADDY. You're not going to introduce me to those men?

DINNY. It's business, Paddy.

SEAN AS PADDY. Brain-surgery business?

DINNY. That's right. Now I'll have to go out to my colleagues and talk to them, Paddy. Are you all right in here with these two lovely ladies?

SEAN AS PADDY. Three ladies, Dinny. Let's not forget Mammy just yet.

DINNY. You're right. (*Touching the coffin and sighing.*) Sorry, Paddy.

DINNY *turns away fast and exits the bedroom and into the sitting room at the same time as* BLAKE *enters from the wardrobe wearing a new woman's blonde permed wig. He plays the part of Mrs Cotter,* EILEEN.

BLAKE AS EILEEN (*upset*). Oh Denis!

DINNY. Yes Eileen.

BLAKE AS EILEEN. Where's the body, love?

DINNY. What?

BLAKE AS EILEEN. The coffin, Denis? The coffin.

DINNY. Well, let me explain first . . .

BLAKE AS EILEEN (*calls*). Peter!

DINNY (*to himself*). Shit shit!

> BLAKE AS EILEEN *enters the kitchen and throws his arms around the coffin.*
>
> DINNY *stands looking aghast at the coffin on the table.*

BLAKE AS EILEEN (*crying a little*). Did you know he slept in this box for two months before he . . . Like he had a premonition.

SEAN AS PETER. Really?

BLAKE AS EILEEN. He loved this box. And then to be struck down in his prime!

SEAN AS PETER. Daddy was ninety-six, Eileen.

BLAKE AS EILEEN. Take off the lid, I want to look at him.

> DINNY *stands in the sitting room listening to their conversation. They look into the coffin.*

SEAN AS PETER. Well, there he is. (*Slight pause.*) Bits of him, anyway.

BLAKE AS EILEEN. He went the way he would have liked to though, didn't he, Peter?

SEAN AS PETER. He did.

BLAKE AS EILEEN. Off the coast of Kinsale travelling at 140 miles an hour. The wind in his hair, his little sailor's outfit on. Speeding fast 'til he hits that bloody sea lion. (*Starts to cry.*) The speedboat thrown into the air. The boat travelling through that field, is that right?

SEAN AS PETER. That's right.

BLAKE AS EILEEN. The horse coming from nowhere. He hits the horse at 100-mile an hour sending it careering over a hedge and onto a quiet country road . . .

DINNY *faints from the shock and hits the ground hard.*

Denis!?

SEAN AS PETER. Good God! Is he all right? Who is he anyway?

BLAKE AS EILEEN. Our painter-decorator.

DINNY *comes around.*

Are you all right, Denis pet?

DINNY (*distantly*). Mother . . .

BLAKE AS EILEEN. No, it's me, Eileen.

DINNY. Horse.

BLAKE AS EILEEN. No, I'm not a horse.

DINNY. Mother . . . killed . . . horse.

BLAKE AS EILEEN. No Denis, that's not right, love. Daddy killed horse.

SEAN AS PETER. And horse killed Daddy.

BLAKE AS EILEEN. Help him into the chair, Peter, quick.

DINNY *is 'unconscious' in the armchair as* SEAN AS PETER *and* BLAKE AS JACK *have a covert conversation.*

BLAKE AS JACK. Is Eileen . . .?

SEAN AS PETER. She's in the kitchen looking at Daddy again.

BLAKE AS JACK. Well, what a complete waste of time.

SEAN AS PETER. I know, I know!

BLAKE AS JACK. Filling him with drink, sticking him on that speedboat and to what end?!

SEAN AS PETER. Well, perhaps Eileen has his money? She could have taken it somewhere, couldn't she?

BLAKE AS JACK. I know my wife's face. She knew that your father kept his money in his house but this morning when we turned everything upside down and found nothing! Her face, Peter?! She was devastated, boy!

He takes a can of beer from SEAN AS PETER*'s hands and finishes it.*

SEAN AS PETER. Well, he'd hardly have gotten rid of it, would he?

DINNY *gets up from the armchair and goes to enter the bedroom as* SEAN AS PADDY *tries to exit the bedroom.*

DINNY. What the hell are you doing!?

SEAN AS PADDY. I have to go to the toilet.

DINNY. You can't.

SEAN AS PADDY. I'm bursting!

DINNY. You'll have to do it in there.

SEAN AS PADDY. It's a dining room!

DINNY. Out the window then.

SEAN AS PADDY. In front of the girls?

SEAN *exits the other door and appears in the living room as* PETER.

SEAN AS PETER. Are they your children out there?

DINNY. What?

SEAN AS PETER. In the garden. They're on the putting green outside.

BLAKE AS JACK *walking fast towards the wardrobe.*

BLAKE AS JACK. My putting green, the little shits!

He enters the wardrobe.

SEAN AS PETER. And I've seen some people inside the dining room.

DINNY *freezes*.

BLAKE AS EILEEN *re-enters the living room and heads for the kitchen*.

From the back garden. A man and two women, don't deny it now!

BLAKE AS EILEEN *pulls out the sausage in the pan*.

BLAKE AS EILEEN (*calling, confused*). Denis, love, what is this?

DINNY. Yes, Mrs Cotter.

BLAKE as EILEEN *brings the large sausage and pan inside to the living room*.

BLAKE AS EILEEN. Is this your chicken?

DINNY. I thought you might fancy a little bit of roast chicken after the funeral.

SEAN AS PETER. How did you know we were coming back? You couldn't have possibly known we were going to arrive back this afternoon. You've been eating Eileen and Jack's food, haven't you? (*He grabs the sausage*.) There's nothing you'd like more than having your three friends around, drinking someone else's alcohol and feeding yourselves with somebody else's chicken . . .

DINNY *screams. He grabs the large sausage and flings it against the wall. It disintegrates*.

Long pause as SEAN *and* BLAKE *brace themselves*.

DINNY (*quietly*). It's not working with the sausage. It's not right.

SEAN (*instinctively*). Is any of it?

Immediately, SEAN *regrets saying anything*. DINNY *grabs him by the hair*.

DINNY. What? Say it!

SEAN. Is any of this story real?

DINNY. Don't doubt me. We allow Mister Doubt into this flat and where would we be? Blake?

BLAKE. We'd be outside, Dad.

DINNY (*not liking* BLAKE*'s tone*). Are you getting brave on me too?

BLAKE. I think I might want to go back to Ireland now.

DINNY. Do I not care for you both? The two little boys who followed me over, didn't I take you in and feed you? Little scraps all tired and hungry, wasn't it me who took you in?

BLAKE. Yes, Dad.

DINNY *grabs* BLAKE *by the ear and drags him into the sitting room.* SEAN *stands at the kitchen entrance looking at them.*

DINNY. And the sea, Blake. The sea, the sea, the sea, the sea, the sea . . .

BLAKE. Dad, don't!

DINNY*'s delivery is focused and steady, he speaks it to* BLAKE.

DINNY. The sea it spits me out onto England. I stand on the shore with Ireland on my back and the tide pushing me across the land towards London. I run, Blake.

BLAKE. I know it, Dad.

DINNY. I run the same race a million Irishmen ran. But pockets full of new money and Paddy's keys in my hands with Walworth Road a final destination, a sure thing, a happy ever after. I run. I run right past the cars in the motorways, the trains in their tracks. I run fast towards London. Days and nights they merge into the one memory. Only the running has any matter. Countryside passing through me and a final farewell to the green. And no horizon of London, I see. No towers or flats or big gate to welcome Dinny. Just road signs and not grass under feet anymore but hard grey now. The road signs steering me. Like a little rat caught in a drain. Pushing me further and further to its centre. But what centre? Me and my suit rolling down the motorway with buildings tighter on either side. And tighter and tighter still, Blake, and when they can't get any tighter, taller they grow. With each mile I run, higher they climb and smaller the dot. Higher the buildings and smaller me. I close my eyes from the size of this place. I stop. Stood still then. (*Long pause.*) The noise and running all stopped, Blake. And I'm stood on grass. I look down at my shoes all knackered . . . soles worn from the run. I catch my breath. I can hear my breathing. So it's all quiet, you see. Ssshhhhhhh. (*A pause.*) I smell the roast chicken from my jumper, Blake. Your mother's kiss to me at the door and telling me, 'Leave now.' (*Slight pause.*) And I think of Paddy and Vera. Their little poisoned bodies piled up on the floor back in Mrs Cotter's house in Cork City. And then I think of me and Paddy as children back in the good old days. A day trip to Robert's Cove and Paddy runs into the sea, a big wave taking him, Dad lost in the pub and I wade in and pick the toddler up. It's only a little bit of water we stand in but Paddy's crying like a scared baba. I take him out and wrap him in Dad's towel. I keep him warm, you know. And I feel good when I think of me and the love I have for Paddy. I stand there looking at the green scabby grass of the roundabout and my knackered shoes. Fuck. (*A pause.*) And then what happened, Blake? What then, tell me?

BLAKE *continues, detached.*

BLAKE. And then it starts from the tiniest quiet thing. You can feel the little shakes up through the grass and up through your body now. Noises from the outside start filling you up. Loud car noises. Stood still with cars all wrapped around your head, stood in the middle of the Elephant and the Castle with Walworth Road right there in front of you. Walworth Road and Paddy and Vera's flat. Only the road to run and get inside, to get you safe. You run fast, Dad.

His eyes suddenly fill with tears. He's terrified.

And then the people. They come out from houses and shops and they're after you. Their skin, it falls to the ground and them bodies running you down and wanting to tear you to shreds. From the river they're coming. They come up from the ground. The concrete snaps open and the bodies are up fast. And they're all snapping teeth and grabbing hands they have. Run faster and faster until a thousand green windows reaching up into the sky and Paddy's flat right at the top and it's calling you. Take to the stairs with the other flats teeming out the bodies wanting to grab you down and get ya. The stairs and your speed. Further away from them you move as you climb higher and the flat higher still. Further away they fall as the flat still higher.

BLAKE *can't continue*.

DINNY. And then, Sean?

SEAN. At cloud height you are and looking over all of London with its bodies down below, its tighter-than-tight buildings, its chewed-up grey, them bad people calling you down. In Paddy and Vera's flat and you're looking over all them who want to gobble us up 'til we're no more. Inside and your heart begins to slow now that you have these safe walls. (*A pause*.) At the window and you're looking out past the end of Walworth Road, past where London stretches into the green countryside, past the green and over the sea to Ireland and to Cork and past the River Lee and high up into the estate and our little terraced house. (*Slight pause*.) And there's Mammy standing by the sink washing the dishes in the kitchen. From the window you can see all of this. In Paddy's flat and you're safe.

Long pause. DINNY *embraces* BLAKE.

DINNY. You believe that lie about that cash-register girl tricking Sean?

BLAKE *doesn't answer*. SEAN *looks on*. DINNY *looks at* SEAN *as he holds* BLAKE.

One lie leads to the next and pretty soon them bodies from outside be banging down our door and dragging you down below, Blake. You watch Sean for me, all right?

BLAKE *turns away and walks into the kitchen*.

SEAN *follows him inside*.

DINNY *sits down and begins to moisturise his head and face again*.

When BLAKE *enters the kitchen he goes straight to a drawer and takes out a large kitchen knife.*

SEAN *watches him.*

BLAKE *faces the sitting room ready to re-enter. The knife is meant for* DINNY.

BLAKE. Them bodies won't get us if we leave the flat, Sean?

SEAN. London's not the way he tells it.

BLAKE. You're sure of it? 'Cause I'm ready to finish it, Sean, but you're sure we won't be got by anyone outside?

SEAN. Well, today I spoke to someone.

BLAKE *turns to him.*

A girl in Tesco, Blake. Got all our food and paid her. She knows me 'cause I'm in at ten o'clock every morning getting the same food for the story. She says that she's seen where I live. Asks me what I do. I can't tell her the truth of what we do in here all day so I say that I'm a builder, though I'm no builder. She's talked about Ireland and how she's seen it on the telly, Blake. She talks about the funny colour of the grass and then the sea. I tell her that I like the sea but how I hadn't seen the sea in so long and she says, 'I'll take you to Brighton Beach and we can walk there.' She means it. She definitely means to take me to that place. So I leave sort of in a daze 'cause of the way she talked to me. I picked up the wrong shopping bag and didn't get out of the daze until I got back here and saw that fecking sausage. But her talking to me like that, Blake . . . even besides the great thing she said . . . her just talking so nice to me . . . it got me thinking more than ever . . . It's right that us two leave.

A pause. BLAKE*'s face hardens. He's not happy.*

BLAKE. You talked to someone outside?

SEAN. She's called Hayley.

They suddenly hear 'A Nation Once Again' sung by Paddy Reilly blasting from the tape recorder.

SEAN *walks through the living room through to the bedroom and takes up his position.*

BLAKE *violently slams the knife into the kitchen table.*

He stares angrily in at SEAN.

He enters the living room as EILEEN *and takes up his position.*

Everything as it should be, DINNY *turns off the music.*

BLAKE AS EILEEN. Can you explain this to me, Dinny?

DINNY. I can, Eileen, I can.

SEAN AS PADDY *enters the sitting room fast and races towards the wardrobe.*

SEAN AS PADDY. Sorry, Dinny, but the bladder's packed it in finally!

He enters the wardrobe.

BLAKE AS EILEEN. Who was that?

DINNY. My brother.

BLAKE *enters the bedroom and re-enters the sitting room as* VERA *and walks right across and into the kitchen and picks up a plate of Ryvita sandwiches.*

SEAN AS PETER *re-enters.*

SEAN AS PETER. So that's your brother in the toilet. Who was that?

DINNY. His wife.

SEAN AS PETER. And what is she doing here?

BLAKE as VERA *re-enters with the Ryvita sandwiches.*

BLAKE AS VERA. Just passing around these lovely sandwiches. I know you people could go a whole day without eating, just thinking those heady thoughts with no time for your stomachs. Didn't imagine that Dinny here would find himself in such illustrious company.

SEAN *goes back to the wardrobe.*

BLAKE AS EILEEN. And you made these sandwiches . . . ?

BLAKE AS VERA. Vera. No I didn't actually make them, no. It was Maureen.

BLAKE AS EILEEN. And who's she?

BLAKE AS VERA. Oh she's Dinny's wife!

BLAKE AS EILEEN. And is she . . . ?

BLAKE AS VERA. She's in the dining room, yeah. Sure I'll just get her for ya.

SEAN AS PETER *re-enters*.

SEAN AS PADDY. Well, thank God for that. Had an awful premonition that my hole would finally strike and I'd be lying prostrate on that lovely bathroom floor of yours. Well then!

DINNY. Eileen, this is Paddy the brother and my wife Maureen.

SEAN AS PADDY. Doctor.

BLAKE AS EILEEN. I beg your pardon?

SEAN AS PADDY. Is there a collective term for brain surgeons?

BLAKE AS EILEEN. I've no idea.

SEAN AS PADDY. You know Dinny here was thrown out of school when he was fifteen for smearing a school desk with . . .

DINNY. Thanks for that, Paddy.

SEAN AS PETER. Quite a gathering. With so many people helping surely your little job in the dining room is finished, Denis?

BLAKE AS VERA. What's there to do apart from sit around and grieve. The sandwiches are made, the chicken is cooking. We all just have to settle into a long evening of drinking. Drinking to life and toasting to death.

SEAN AS PETER. Well, that's very kind of you, Vera. It shows a beautiful character. Someone who can reach out to a stranger who's lost a parent.

BLAKE AS VERA (*covertly*). Can you see that?

SEAN AS PETER. Well, it's obvious.

BLAKE AS VERA. A stranger really?

SEAN AS PETER. Of course.

BLAKE AS VERA. You're right, you know. Do you think in eight years of marriage a person can end up a stranger with their own husband?

SEAN AS PETER. Well, that's an altogether different matter.

DINNY (*in mid-conversation*). . . . and Maureen knowing of this imminent gathering thought to prepare some finger food for us all.

BLAKE AS EILEEN. Maureen, that's very kind of you.

DINNY. Kind? Sure she lives for the kitchen!

BLAKE AS EILEEN. Even somebody else's kitchen, Maureen?

A pause as BLAKE AS MAUREEN *looks flustered.* DINNY *thrown.*

BLAKE AS MAUREEN. I'll get on with that chicken so!

DINNY. Great stuff, Maureen! Thanks, love.

BLAKE AS MAUREEN *walks into the kitchen, sees the open coffin and audibly gasps.*

DINNY *races into her.*

BLAKE AS MAUREEN (*whispering*). How did Mammy get over here?

DINNY. That's not Mammy. It's Mrs Cotter's father, look.

BLAKE AS MAUREEN (*looking inside*). What's he doing there?

DINNY. What do you think?! He's dead. Now stay put and cook, Maureen. Cook your little heart out! Get people's mouths full and they won't be able to speak, right.

DINNY *exits into the sitting room.*

BLAKE *exits into the stage right wardrobe.*

SEAN AS PADDY. Lovely people, Dinny! You'd imagine brain surgeons all stuffy. But nothing like it. She's lovely, Eileen! Said you were a great worker and that I could learn a lot from you . . . 'Though one brain surgeon in the family is enough, thank you very much, Eileen!' And look how that Peter fella's chatting up my Vera and getting close to her. Real charming bunch, aren't they? Christ it's shaping up into a lovely day!

BLAKE AS JACK *enters through the wardrobe.*

BLAKE AS JACK. Are these your two little boys, Denis!?

DINNY. Well, that depends, Mr Cotter . . .

BLAKE AS JACK. I walk out to the garden and they've got a neighbourhood child, Finbarr, pinned to the putting green. A great big bloody arm on him, Eileen. He's spread-eagled and knocked unconscious by these two little brats who are just about to do the unspeakable.

DINNY. Blake, explain this to me now?! Sean, come on.

SEAN. He was all by himself with his dog Bouncer and we thought it would be fun if he played with us.

BLAKE. Finbarr's in the scouts and came back with his tent so we could play soldiers.

SEAN. He told us about survival and how he was being trained to survive in the wild.

DINNY. What age is this boy?

BLAKE. Six.

DINNY. Carry on.

SEAN. So he's bragging, Dad. He's bragging about surviving in the wild, about pissing on snake bites when a snake does bite. And all this time he's unpacking his tent.

BLAKE. No tent in there, Dad. Just poles and pins.

SEAN. So I says that maybe he should be the tent. Maybe we should pin down Finbarr and stick a pole up his centre and keep cover under him.

BLAKE. We pin him down and he starts to cry like a baby and not the bush man he makes himself out to be. Sets his big dog on us. Now Sean's afraid of dogs, that's right, isn't it, Dad?

DINNY. He is, yeah.

BLAKE. So I pick up a pole and start on Bouncer to protect my little brother.

DINNY. Good man, Blake.

BLAKE. Give him a few whacks on the back and he's getting fierce angry.

SEAN. And all the time we're sort of dancing over 'Finbarr the tent' on the ground. When all of a sudden . . .

BLAKE. Snap!

SEAN. Terrible noise, Dad.

BLAKE. I look down and see Finbarr's little arm in Bouncer's mouth.

SEAN. He's only six so he's got every right to fall unconscious, Dad.

BLAKE. I take the tent pole and one last swipe, I fire it right up Bouncer's arse. He's away like a bat of hell with the pole still dangling out his rear end and here we are with Finbarr's bloody arm needing some serious attention.

SEAN. Well, all this talk of being out in the wild and surviving on the basics and what we did next just seemed liked the most natural.

BLAKE. Looking at his broken arm we decided to give it the snake bite treatment.

SEAN. So we pissed on him.

A pause.

DINNY *turns to 'the others' and shrugs his shoulders.*

DINNY. Fair play.

SEAN *enters the kitchen as* PETER.

BLAKE *enters the kitchen as* JACK.

BLAKE AS JACK (*furiously*). For Christ's sake, Peter. We shouldn't have bothered murdering this old shit.

He grabs a can beer from SEAN*'s hand.*

SEAN AS PETER. Keep your voice down, Jack.

BLAKE AS JACK *drains the can of beer, much to* SEAN AS PETER*'s annoyance.*

BLAKE AS JACK. For all his money your father's worthless to us. This coffin is worth more than him.

BLAKE AS JACK *pulls up the pillow.*

This ridiculous plump lining.

He starts to bang the pillow off the coffin.

Jesus the extravagance of the man. This silk bloody pillow with his initials on it for GOD'S SAKE!! I MEAN . . .

Suddenly the pillow tears and Monopoly money is thrown in the air.

Suddenly the doorbell makes a continuous buzzing sound.

The three of them freeze.

The doorbell stops.

Instinctively, BLAKE *grabs a kitchen knife to protect himself.*

BLAKE *and* SEAN *come out to the sitting room and look at the front door.*

The doorbell sounds again.

BLAKE *and* SEAN *look to their father. He points to* BLAKE *to open it.*

With huge trepidation BLAKE *walks towards the front door and begins to undo the many locks.*

He then opens the door and steps way back as he holds the kitchen knife.

It's raining outside and standing in the rain is a twenty-four-year-old black woman holding a Tesco bag.

The three just stare at her.

This is HAYLEY.

HAYLEY (*hesitantly*). Is Sean in? It's just he took the wrong shopping. This is his one.

The three just look at her.

HAYLEY *then recognises* SEAN.

Hey Sean! It's me, Hayley.

SEAN *wants to disappear. He looks at the floor.*

She enters out of the rain. BLAKE *moves back from her.*

A pause.

Hey.

DINNY. Is there a cooked chicken and sliced pan in there?

HAYLEY. Yeah. And two packets of pink wafers and . . . well what you usually get.

A pause.

DINNY. Can you cook?

HAYLEY. Why? Is this like *Ready Steady Cook* or something?! Only you don't look like Ainsley Harriott!

She laughs.

DINNY *just stares through her and waits for her to stop laughing.*

She stops laughing.

DINNY. Can you cook?

HAYLEY *a little awkward now.*

HAYLEY. Yeah.

HAYLEY *stands as the three just stare at her for a long time and the rain continues outside.*

Loud guttural rhythmic music fades up and fills the stage and auditorium.

The music continues to build, the stage reverberating and unable to take its noise.

Blackout.

Silence.

Curtain Falls.

End of Act One.

ACT TWO

The curtain rises quickly.

DINNY *stands in the centre of the sitting room staring towards the kitchen.*

BLAKE *stands near him also looking towards the kitchen where* HAYLEY *and* SEAN *are talking.*

The nervous and talkative HAYLEY *has her coat off and wears a Tesco uniform.*

SEAN*'s naturally very anxious about her being inside their flat.*

HAYLEY*'s staring into the coffin.*

HAYLEY. That's a big box. What are you using it for? Looks like a coffin.

SEAN. It's just cardboard.

HAYLEY. I tell you, after them stairs, I could climb right in there for a little nap. What we up here? Fourteen floors . . .

SEAN. Fifteen.

HAYLEY. Fifteen floors with no lift! You should get on to the Council. Took me ten minutes to get up. I'm a pretty fit girl. I play football down Burgess Park. Well try . . . I'm not bad . . . But the important thing is to keep healthy. Do you do anything to keep fit?

SEAN (*distracted*). I do a bit of running.

HAYLEY. You get a decent workout from those stairs. Every morning at ten o'clock, up with your shopping.

SEAN. Yeah.

DINNY *gestures to* BLAKE *to pay attention to* HAYLEY.

BLAKE *stands by the kitchen entrance looking inside at her.*

HAYLEY. A creature of habit, aren't you? Oven-cooked chicken, white sliced bread, yeah? . . . Creamy milk, two packets of pink wafers, six cans of Harp and one cheesy spread. The other girls think you're an idiot but I was saying that there's a lot of sense to it. All the options that people have these days . . . it's all very confusing. If you're happy with your lifestyle and what you eat, why change?

During the following exchange, BLAKE *begins to mimic* HAYLEY*'s gestures, walk, stance. He's practising being her.*

Unaware of this, HAYLEY *suddenly notices the money on the kitchen floor.*

Is that Monopoly money?

SEAN. Yeah.

HAYLEY. Lively game was it? A bit messy in here. Is it just the three of you? Your brother and dad and you. No mother?

SEAN. She lives in Ireland.

HAYLEY. Divorced are they?

SEAN. No.

HAYLEY. Won't she come over? Doesn't she like London?

SEAN. I don't know.

HAYLEY. When you last see her?

SEAN. When I was five.

HAYLEY. Shut up! That's terrible. Five, really? Christ. Gotta get back and see her, Sean. Do you miss her?

SEAN. Yeah.

HAYLEY. Is she nice?

SEAN. She's a good cook.

HAYLEY. Aw you miss her cooking. How sweet. Why's your brother dressed like that?

SEAN. Like what?

HAYLEY. Like a woman. He's a transvestite, right?

SEAN. Ah what?

HAYLEY. He likes women's clothes.

SEAN. No it's a joke. He's just joking, that's all.

HAYLEY. I wouldn't mind if he was a transvestite.

SEAN. He's not.

HAYLEY. Well, I wouldn't mind if he was. It's a free world.

SEAN. He's a joker.

HAYLEY. He's a builder as well is he?

SEAN. Yeah a builder.

HAYLEY. So no building work today? Just chilling out?
Playing Monopoly. Taking it easy. Fooling around.

SEAN. Yeah.

HAYLEY. And dressing up in women's clothes?!

SEAN. Just Blake.

HAYLEY. The joker.

SEAN *looks back to the sitting room.*

Didn't know you were bald by the way. You always wear
that cute hat all the time. Looks like you shave it too. Is it a
fashion statement or something 'cause I quite like bald men.
Trying to impress me?

She laughs a little. She's flirting with him.

Sorry I'm talking so much. My mum reckons it's from
working at Tesco. You talk all day to the customers, get
home and I can't stop talking. It's not intentional! You get
stuck in a pattern. Christ, you've no idea what I mean, do
you?

SEAN. No I know what you mean.

HAYLEY. So was he serious? Your dad. He really wants me to
fix his lunch the way he said?

SEAN. He does, yeah.

HAYLEY. A bit rich though isn't it? I'm on my lunch break, I come up here as a favour and end up fixing his lunch.

SEAN. You've been very nice.

HAYLEY. Well, that's the Tesco training. It's all about customer care.

SEAN. Thank you.

HAYLEY. Thank you and have a nice day!

SEAN (*confused*). Okay.

HAYLEY. S'pose if I might get something out of it though?

She takes a can of Harp out of the Tesco bag and smiles.

A bit early but . . . after them stairs and . . .

She opens the can of beer.

DINNY *fires a look over at the kitchen as he hears the can open.*

HAYLEY *drinks some beer.*

BLAKE *does a perfect impersonation of* HAYLEY.

BLAKE. Looks like you shave it too. Are you trying to impress me?

HAYLEY *quickly turns and sees* BLAKE *looking in at her. She's a little nervous of him.*

HAYLEY. Very good. (*As* SEAN *takes her to one side.*) Why's he looking at me like that?

SEAN. Be honest with me please. Why did you come here?

A pause.

HAYLEY. To be nice. To do a nice thing.

A pause.

SEAN (*anxious*). But for no other reason, Hayley? Something you won't tell me?

HAYLEY. How d'you mean?

SEAN. Not to trick me?

HAYLEY's a little confused. She just laughs.

HAYLEY. Seriously?

DINNY puts on the tape recorder and 'An Irish Lullaby' begins to play.

SEAN *tenses up. It can only mean one thing.*

(*Of the music.*) That sounds nice. Quite old fashioned but I quite like that. (*Slight pause. Closes her eyes.*) Green grass. Stone walls. A little thatched cottage by the river. Little girl with red hair in ringlets sat on a donkey. (*Opening her eyes.*) Does it remind you of back home in Ireland?

SEAN. No.

A pause. She can see that SEAN looks frightened of something.

HAYLEY. I'm not here to trick you, Sean, honest.

She tugs at his sleeve playfully.

All right?

Seeing this, BLAKE enters fast and takes SEAN by the hand in an act of possession.

HAYLEY *backs away from them.*

Well, I suppose I'll get his lunch on then.

The music continues.

HAYLEY *prepares the lunch.*

DINNY *stands up and puts his wig back on and grooms himself in preparation.*

BLAKE *gathers up the Monopoly money, refills and resets the pillow into the coffin.*

SEAN *looks terrified.*

Suddenly DINNY slams the tape recorder off.

BLAKE *and SEAN race into the sitting room.*

The Farce resumes with pace. BLAKE *and* SEAN *are playing their younger selves.*

BLAKE. He's away like a bat of hell with the pole still dangling out his rear end and here we are with Finbarr's bloody arm needing some serious attention, Dad.

SEAN (*lowering his voice so* HAYLEY *doesn't hear*). Well all this talk of being out in the wild and surviving on the basics and what we did next just seemed the most natural.

BLAKE. Looking at his broken arm we decided to give it the snake bite treatment.

SEAN. So we pissed on him.

DINNY. Fair play.

BLAKE *grabs* SEAN *and quickly enters the kitchen with him.*

HAYLEY *turns to them.*

HAYLEY. D'you have any salt?

BLAKE AS JACK (*furious*). For Christ's sake, Peter. We shouldn't have bothered murdering this old shit.

He takes a can of beer from SEAN*'s hand.*

SEAN AS PETER. Keep your voice down, Jack.

BLAKE AS JACK (*draining the can of beer*). For all his money your father's worthless to us. This coffin is worth more than him.

BLAKE *pulls up the pillow.*

This ridiculous plump lining.

BLAKE *starts banging the pillow off the coffin.*

HAYLEY. Sean?

BLAKE AS JACK. Jesus the extravagance of the man. This silk bloody pillow with his initials on it for GOD'S SAKE!! I MEAN . . .

The pillow rips.

SEAN, BLAKE *and* HAYLEY *freeze as the Monopoly money falls around them.*

HAYLEY (*smiling*). Is this some sort of joke?

BLAKE *pulls* SEAN'*s arm and drags him back into the sitting room.*

DINNY. All right, boys, back in the back garden and behave yourself.

SEAN *and* BLAKE *disappear into the right wardrobe and reappear fast as* PADDY *and* EILEEN.

SEAN AS PADDY. Christ, Dinny, they're a handful, them kids. They wouldn't be my idea of children now.

HAYLEY *stands at the kitchen entrance. She's beginning to laugh at what's happening.*

DINNY. They wouldn't?

SEAN AS PADDY. I'd be of the thinking that children should be seen and not heard. Unless of course it was a children's choral choir in which case seeing and hearing would be an absolute delight.

HAYLEY *laughs a little.*

DINNY. Not at all, Paddy. Sure look at us. Raucous were we not? More than a handful. Two handfuls.

BLAKE AS EILEEN (*dreamily*). Bit of fighter were you, Denis?

DINNY. I was, Eileen. Back in the days when Cork City was dog rough, where to take a night-time stroll was an act of madness comparable to forcing long deadly skewers into your eyeballs, Cork was a jungle back then. And I'm not saying that I was its Tarzan . . .

SEAN AS PADDY. Because you can't swim.

DINNY. That's right, you're right. But I was more in the mode of King Kong, if you get my meaning. A gigantic freakish gorilla, intent on protecting his own and causing untold damage and chaos to those who challenge my jungle authority.

SEAN *looks towards* HAYLEY.

HAYLEY (*smiling*). It's good.

BLAKE AS EILEEN *gets closer to* DINNY.

BLAKE AS EILEEN (*whispering*). If only Jack had the same primal strength, the same domination.

DINNY (*whispering*). I know in this hour of grief I must be a symbol of reliability and power to you, Eileen. But I must warn you . . . flattery will get you into everywhere.

DINNY *and* BLAKE AS EILEEN *share a flirtatious laugh.*

BLAKE *and* SEAN *enter the kitchen fast, making* HAYLEY *step back into it.*

BLAKE AS JACK (*picking up the money*). How much do you think is here, Peter?

SEAN AS PETER. All of it maybe. These are big notes, Jack.

BLAKE AS JACK. Get it back in the coffin quick.

They gather up the money and shove it in the coffin.

HAYLEY. Can you stop just for a sec . . .

SEAN AS PETER. So what's our plan, Jack?

BLAKE AS JACK. Plan, plan, plan?! He stays here tonight. Tomorrow, me and you get him back in the hearse and drive. We pull over in a lay-by, divide the cash and get on with our new lives. Feck it, the sooner I leave that Eileen bitch and start to express myself the better!

SEAN AS PETER. Ah now that's my sister you're talking about, Jack.

BLAKE AS JACK. Oh the family man, are ya?! Filling your daddy with two bottles of gin, a bag of glue and strapping him into that speedboat, remember!

BLAKE AS JACK *grabs his beer and knocks it back.*

SEAN AS PETER (*peeved*). Why do you keep on taking my drink like that!?

DINNY (*explaining to* HAYLEY). Greedy Jack always hungry for the drink! Snatching it away at the last moment. Good detail, lads! We'll explain that in the finish! (*Prompting*.) Again, Blake, again!

BLAKE AS JACK. Filling your daddy with two bottles of gin, a bag of glue and strapping him into that speedboat, remember!

BLAKE AS JACK *grabs his beer and knocks it back*.

SEAN AS PETER (*peeved*). Why do you keep on taking my drink like that!?

DINNY. Excellent, boys!

BLAKE AS MAUREEN. Is everyone going to have chicken?

SEAN AS PETER *and* BLAKE AS JACK (*a scream*). Ahhh!

HAYLEY (*annoyed*). Hellooooooooo!

BLAKE AS JACK (*whispering*). Who the hell's that?

SEAN AS PETER (*whispering*). The painter's wife, Maureen.

BLAKE AS JACK. Shit. Shit! (*Addressing* MAUREEN.) How much of that did you hear, Maureen?

BLAKE AS MAUREEN. Hearse. Lay-by. Dividing the cash.

BLAKE AS JACK. Well, it is ours.

BLAKE AS MAUREEN. What about Mrs Cotter?

SEAN AS PETER. Her husband Jack here's looking after her share.

HAYLEY. Right, I'm off then, Sean!

BLAKE AS JACK. It's not like it's any of your business anyway, Maureen.

HAYLEY. Sean!

SEAN AS PETER. It'll be our little secret then, Maureen?

BLAKE AS MAUREEN. I'll get on with the food so.

Irritated, HAYLEY *grabs her coat and bag and leaves the kitchen and heads for the front door.*

50

DINNY *looks at her as she tries to open the locks on the door.*

HAYLEY (*exasperated*). Oh open the fucking door!

DINNY *suddenly pounces on her and grabs her by the throat, pinning her to the door. He takes her bag and throws it to one side.*

SEAN *and* BLAKE *come out from the kitchen and stand by, watching.*

DINNY. Don't scream now.

HAYLEY, *terrified, looks towards* SEAN.

Here to break us up, boys. Trick us and drag us down to the street.

HAYLEY (*quietly*). What?

DINNY. Just do what I asked and you won't be hurt.

HAYLEY*'s eyes fill with tears.*

HAYLEY. But what are you doing?

A pause.

Why are you all doing this?

A pause as DINNY *just looks at her.*

DINNY. You be a good girl, take off your coat and do what I asked ya.

BLAKE *helps her off with her coat and immediately puts it on. Again he perfectly impersonates her.*

BLAKE. Thank you and have a nice day!

HAYLEY (*to* SEAN). Do something, Sean!

DINNY *turns* SEAN *towards him.*

DINNY. 'Feck it, Dinny, I don't . . .'

SEAN. Dad, please . . .

DINNY. 'Feck it, Dinny . . .'

SEAN. We can't keep her like this!

BLAKE. SAY IT, SEAN! SAY IT!

BLAKE and DINNY *side by side wait for* SEAN *to get back on track.*

SEAN *looks back at* HAYLEY.

HAYLEY. Please.

Then, slowly:

SEAN AS PADDY. Feck it, Dinny, I don't like that Peter fella at all! Closer he's getting to my Vera and the way he's looking down at me . . .

DINNY. Easy, Paddy. It's a walk in the garden you need.

HAYLEY *walks back into the kitchen as the three just look at her.*

Again, Sean! Come on! Come on!

SEAN AS PADDY (*more energy*). Feck it, Dinny, I don't like that Peter fella at all! Closer he's getting to my Vera and the way he's looking down at me . . .

DINNY. Easy, Paddy. It's a walk in the garden you need.

SEAN AS PADDY. I understand the stress you brain surgeons are under but I don't see you patronising me like that.

DINNY. Good man, Sean!

SEAN AS PADDY. You're not embarrassed of me are you?

DINNY. What?

BLAKE *takes off* HAYLEY*'s coat and drops it on the floor. He stands at the kitchen entrance looking in at her.*

SEAN AS PADDY. Embarrassed of me. Tell me straight, are ya, Dinny?

DINNY. Embarrassed of you? Embarrassed of my own little brother? A man who lives in abject poverty in a hovel in London. A brother so ugly that when he was born, the doctors thought our mother had pushed out her perforated poisoned liver. A man who as a boy was so unpopular that even his imaginary friends would beat him up. A brother so stupid that for twenty years he thought that Irish dancing was a running event for people who were afraid to travel.

SEAN AS PADDY. You're not embarrassed of me then?

DINNY *gives him a look.*

DINNY. Keep an eye on Blake and Sean for us, Paddy, and make sure they don't torture anything.

SEAN AS PADDY. Righty ho!

SEAN *enters the right wardrobe. From inside an enormous scream of anguish:*

SEAN. FUCK!

BLAKE *and* DINNY *look towards the wardrobe and* DINNY *starts to laugh.*

DINNY. Good, Blake.

BLAKE. Thanks, Dad.

DINNY. Off ya go, son.

BLAKE *quickly puts on* EILEEN's *wig and walks into the bedroom and sees the coffin.*

BLAKE AS EILEEN. Oh my God what's this?!

SEAN *arrives fast as* PETER, *and, seeing the coffin:*

SEAN AS PETER. What the hell?!

BLAKE AS EILEEN. Who is that?

SEAN AS PETER. What's that smell of whiskey?

DINNY. It's my mother.

BLAKE AS EILEEN. What's your mother doing on my dining-room table, Denis?

DINNY. She's dead.

BLAKE AS EILEEN. You bring your dead mother on jobs with you?

SEAN AS PETER. You're using my sister's house for your dead mother's wake! You sneak!

BLAKE AS EILEEN. Oh, Denis . . .

DINNY (*snaps*). It's for Paddy! I know I shouldn't be here but I was doing it all for Paddy . . . because of his . . . condition.

BLAKE AS EILEEN. What condition, Denis?

A pause.

DINNY. Paddy's fallen on rough times, Eileen. Him and his wife Vera live destitute in a towerblock in London.

BLAKE AS EILEEN. So?

DINNY (*obviously thinking on his feet*). One day last year . . . Paddy, cold and shivering . . . walked down the Walworth Road and into a pet shop for some warmth. He was in there looking at the guppies in their tanks and talking to the budgies in their cages. The owner figured out that he was a retard so he let him at it.

BLAKE AS EILEEN (*lost*). Okay.

DINNY. Now Paddy was ravenous with the hunger. The last bit of solid to pass his lips was the nib of a bookie's pen and that was a whole week ago. There in the back of the pet shop, slunked in the corner . . . in an old crate . . . was a giant snake . . . called . . . the . . . (*Thinks hard.*) . . . Big . . . Langer Snake . . . eating a carrot. Well, Paddy, God bless him, didn't give it much thought, reached in and grabbed that Langer's dinner. When SNAP! Paddy was bitten and infected with a terrible snake venom.

BLAKE AS EILEEN. So is he dying?

DINNY. He will die, yeah. In the meantime his infected brain has started an unrelenting rot.

SEAN AS PETER. That would explain all his brain-surgeon nonsense.

DINNY. I took him here as a special treat, honest, Eileen. We were meant to bury Mammy today but Paddy wouldn't part with her. You arrived with your terrible news about your dead daddy and for some reason . . . Paddy's convinced that you're all brain surgeons intent on removing that snake venom from his miniscule brain.

Slight pause.

BLAKE AS EILEEN. I might have known that your reasons were for reasons of love. It's a wonderful thing to see such a bond between two family members.

SEAN AS PETER (*with true regret*). It's not always the case with us, is it, Eileen?

BLAKE AS EILEEN. With Denis's inspiration . . . I'm sure we can change, little brother.

A slight pause.

DINNY (*with relief and immense self-satisfaction*). Well, I don't know about you two but I could murder a drink!

DINNY *pops open a well-earned can of Harp.*

BLAKE AS JACK. I've been in the kitchen counting all the money. We're looking at fifty grand each, Peter!

SEAN AS PETER. I'm starting to feel uneasy about this.

BLAKE AS JACK. Uneasy?! Uneasy?! What do you mean?

SEAN AS PETER. Orchestrating Daddy's death was one thing but I can't stab my own sister in the back. It's her money too, Jack.

BLAKE AS JACK (*grabbing* SEAN AS PETER). Listen to me, you little shit! We had a deal. You've seen how she's treated me. Bullied in my own home so I have to spend my days sneaking around in the garden shed and drinking methylated spirits to keep myself sane!

SEAN AS PETER. Yes I . . .

BLAKE AS JACK. I deserve that money, you said so yourself. You back out on me now and I'll make shit of you, do you hear me! I'll have you, Peter. You and your sister, I swear it, man!

SEAN AS PETER. Oh Jack, come on!

BLAKE AS JACK *suddenly smacks* SEAN AS PETER *hard across the face. A little too hard.*

SEAN, *taken aback, dives at* BLAKE. *The two fall to the ground and start to fight each other.*

DINNY *nonchalantly walks past them and over to the kitchen and* HAYLEY.

He looks at her for some time.

DINNY. How's my chicken coming along?

A slight pause.

HAYLEY. It's heating in the oven.

DINNY. A lovely smell . . . roasting chicken.

HAYLEY *remains quiet.*

DINNY *drinks from his can of Harp.*

Thirsty work this. Drama piling on, isn't it?

HAYLEY. Yeah.

DINNY. Impressive work. Wonderful detail. (*A pause.*) Who d'you reckon has the best chance with the acting trophy today? Me is it? I'd be the best one, would I? Don't be shy!

HAYLEY. I suppose.

A pause.

DINNY. You're black. What are we going to do about that, Maureen?

DINNY *continues to drink his can of Harp and look at her.*

BLAKE *has* SEAN *on the ground and is strangling him.*

Realising what he's doing, BLAKE *stops. He remains sitting on* SEAN's *chest looking down on him.*

BLAKE (*quietly*). Were you talking to her about us? Are you trying to find ways to get us down to the streets? Send the little girl up and the door starts banging with more bodies wanting to get us. Are you turning your back on me, Sean?

DINNY *stands at the kitchen entrance looking in on the two of them.*

SEAN. I wouldn't do that. I couldn't be alone outside without you, Blake.

BLAKE. But you're wanting me to kill Dad, aren't you, Sean? We kill Dad, break the story, step outside like you've got it all planned . . . but then you walk away from me with her.

SEAN. With her?

BLAKE. You love her, tell me.

SEAN. Blake, we can both leave here. Me and you.

BLAKE. You can't deny you love her!

SEAN. You don't have to be scared of what's out there anymore.

BLAKE. WE BELONG IN HERE!

SEAN. Blake . . .

BLAKE slaps him hard across the face.

He climbs off SEAN and stands over him.

BLAKE. You break what I know and I give you my word, little brother, I'll have to kill you. (*Less sure.*) I can kill you straight.

SEAN. Then you'll live with what he lives with . . .

BLAKE. It's not true.

SEAN. I saw him, Blake. I saw the blood that day! It's all lies!

BLAKE. It was Mr Cotter and the poisoned chicken . . .

SEAN. Jesus, Blake . . .

BLAKE. No, Sean, no! No no no no!

SEAN. Blake!

BLAKE covers his ears and enters the bedroom and lies on the bed with his head beneath the pillow.

SEAN remains lying on the floor. He then notices DINNY standing looking down at him. He must have heard what he just said.

DINNY. All a little bit fucked today, isn't it, Sean?

SEAN. Yes, Dad.

DINNY. Come here to me so.

DINNY *walks back inside the kitchen.*

SEAN *gets up and walks inside too.*

HAYLEY *stands at the cooker and* DINNY *sits at the table.*
SEAN *stands by the entrance.*

A pause.

Tell me what you remember the day I left Cork, Sean.

SEAN. Why?

DINNY. Well, is it the same as the way we tell it?

A pause.

SEAN. No.

A pause.

DINNY. No? (*He's angry but keeps calm. A pause.*) Let me
hear it so I can see where I stand with ya. You're playing in
Mrs Cotter's back garden.

SEAN (*a pause*). No, Dad. We're playing in our back garden
me and Blake. Granny's coffin's open in the front room and
the room smells of dust so you send us out into the fresh air.
We're lying on the grass and we're talking about what we'll
be when we're all grown up. Blake full of talk about being
an astronaut. He's read a book on it and he knows some big
words to do with space. He says he'd feel safe up there. He
said if he got nervous he'd hide the Earth behind his thumb.
He talked about a parade in Dublin when the space men got
back from space. How there'd have to be a special parade
for him in Cork and everyone would come out and cheer
him on and slag off the Dubs. We're just sitting on the grass
chatting like that. (*A pause.*) I say I want to be a bus driver
because I like buses and Blake thinks that it's a great job.
Just like driving a rocket 'cept your orbit's the Grand
Parade and Mac Curtain Street. (*A pause.*) There's shouting
from inside the house. You and Uncle Paddy screaming at

each other. Fighting over Granny's money even before she's stuck in the ground. Aunty Vera crying her cries real high like a baby crying. Your voice so much bigger than Uncle Paddy and him saying, 'No, Dinny, no please, Dinny!' (*Slight pause.*) And then we hear Mammy screaming, Dad. We're both up fast and running through our back door and into our kitchen and the smell of the roast chicken. Her screaming coming from the sitting room and Blake won't go inside 'cause he's frightened of what he might see. But I do. I do go inside. And Mammy grabs me and spins me around fast so I can't see . . . but I see Uncle Paddy and Aunty Vera on the ground and I see you standing in the corner with blood all over your hands. There's blood on your hands and a kitchen knife, I'm sure of it. (*A pause.*) Mam's terrible screaming. And you're standing at the door and I can see that you're trying to make up your mind whether to stay or to run. And Mammy kisses you and says, 'Leave, now', and sets you free. You just step out to the outside and begin your run.

A long pause.

DINNY. Why did your mammy send you two little boys right after me if I did a bad thing?

SEAN. Because she still loved you. Because what we had used to be so good in Ireland. Maybe she could forgive you. (*Slight pause.*) Dad, I don't know why she sent us.

A pause.

Momentarily, DINNY *is affected by what* SEAN *says.*

DINNY. I'm keeping you and Blake safe.

SEAN. I know you think that.

DINNY (*aggravated now*). FUCK!!

HAYLEY *flinches.*

(*Quickly.*) So what did you two talk about?

DINNY *turns* HAYLEY *around to face him.*

You talked this morning in Tesco, didn't you? Talkin' about what we get up to in here, Sean?

SEAN. No, Dad.

DINNY places SEAN *opposite* HAYLEY.

DINNY. Don't be lying to me and tell me what was said. Show me exactly how it was. The same words. Play it. (*To* HAYLEY.) Sit down!

He sits HAYLEY *down by the table.*

(*To* SEAN.) You walk up to her and you say:

HAYLEY. All right?

DINNY. And you say what then?

SEAN. Hello.

DINNY. Do the shopping, come on, come on!

HAYLEY *mimes scanning* SEAN*'s shopping.*

DINNY *mimes packing the shopping into a plastic bag.*

(*To* HAYLEY.) And you say?

HAYLEY. Same shopping as usual? (*Breaks.*) Look, please let me leave!

DINNY (*snaps*). Again again!

HAYLEY. Same shopping as usual?

SEAN. And I laugh a little for no good reason. (*Slight pause. To* HAYLEY.) I'm so sorry.

HAYLEY *breaks down again.*

DINNY *shakes her to talk. A pause as she controls herself.*

HAYLEY. Are you doing anything at the weekend? It's just I might go down to Brighton Beach, have you ever been there?

SEAN. No.

HAYLEY. It's nice. Maybe you'd like to go there with me sometime.

BLAKE *appears out of the bedroom and stands listening to* SEAN *and* HAYLEY *talking in the kitchen.*

SEAN. And I can't say anything as I pack the shopping away. (*Slight pause.*) But I'm thinking of whether I could ever risk my life with somebody else. If there would ever come a time when someone would promise me a new start. I'm thinking about us walking on a beach by the sea and I'm wondering if you'd stay with me if I got outside, Hayley. But you can't see me thinking about all of that. And I want to say, 'I'd really like to go there one day.'

HAYLEY *almost smiles.*

HAYLEY. Then I would say, 'Let's go, Sean. Let's leave now.'

A slight pause.

SEAN (*quietly*). You would?

BLAKE *hits the play button on the tape recorder and 'A Nation Once Again' blares loudly out.*

He starts to thrash the flat.

DINNY *goes to the sitting room to see him. He starts to laugh.*

DINNY. Good man, Blake! That a boy! Go on now! Go on, Blake!

Everything's unravelling.

SEAN *looks very worried. Suddenly he notices* HAYLEY*'s holding his hand.*

She gestures that her phone is in her bag in the sitting room and that SEAN *should get it.*

DINNY *turns and grabs* SEAN *and throws him out into the sitting room.*

BLAKE *continues demolishing the flat as* SEAN *watches him.*

DINNY *turns off the music.*

(*Snaps.*) Enough, Blake!

BLAKE *stops. He stares at* SEAN, *strikes him hard across the face.*

SEAN *hits the ground*.

BLAKE AS JACK (*announcing*). Anyone care where I am . . . I'm in the garden shed!

BLAKE AS JACK *walks quickly away and enters a wardrobe and closes the door.*

DINNY (*threatening* SEAN). You back down, do you hear me?

BLAKE *re-enters fast as* VERA *and heads for* SEAN AS PETER *as he gets up.*

BLAKE AS VERA. Did Jack hurt you, Peter love? You had an argument, did ya?! I know what you science types are like. Fierce competitive. Good Christ, I like your style! You make my Paddy look like another species.

SEAN AS PETER (*dazed*). I can't understand what you're doing with Paddy, Vera. Having loyalty to a man with his condition.

BLAKE AS VERA. Sure Paddy's hole is only a part of his problem.

SEAN AS PETER. What a beautiful lady you are.

BLAKE AS VERA. At last someone to scoop me up in their arms and ride me horse back down Walworth Road to sunnier and better climes!

SEAN *returns to the wardrobe.*

DINNY (*walking into the bedroom, mid-conversation*). I hear what you're saying, Eileen, but I've only got so much love to spread about, darling.

BLAKE AS EILEEN. But that wife of yours!

DINNY. Boring she might be. The personality of a dead fish, she most certainly has, but what Maureen can do in the kitchen. Like a wizard in there.

BLAKE AS EILEEN. But in the bedroom, Denis? How is she in the bedroom.

DINNY. She can give as good as she gets.

BLAKE AS EILEEN. You see that's the sort of talk I like to hear from a real man!

DINNY. Oh now, Eileen, please! There's one thing cheating on my unsuspecting and stupid wife and another thing entirely bringing disgrace on my dear mother as she lies in her eternal sleep.

SEAN *opens the wardrobe door to sneak out into the room and get* HAYLEY*'s bag.*

BLAKE AS EILEEN. Such a strange expression she has on her face, Denis.

BLAKE AS EILEEN *looks in the coffin,*

DINNY. She has. As if she's bitten into a lemon.

BLAKE AS EILEEN. Not the sort of face you want to wear in eternal life.

DINNY. That's true . . . but the poor love didn't have a choice. Reconstructed her head and face was . . . Hang on a sec . . .

SEAN *is back in the wardrobe fast as* DINNY *walks from the bedroom through the sitting room and into the kitchen.*

(*Glancing at* HAYLEY.) Carry on, carry on!

He takes up a washing-up-liquid bottle and fills it with water.

He returns to the bedroom with the bottle and takes up his position.

Again, Blake.

BLAKE AS EILEEN. Such a strange expression she has on her face, Denis.

DINNY. She has. As if she's bitten into a lemon, Eileen.

BLAKE AS EILEEN. Not the sort of face you want to wear in eternal life.

DINNY. That's true . . . but the poor love didn't have a choice. Reconstructed her head and face was but . . .

He squirts some water from the bottle into his eyes to effect tears.

(*Getting emotional.*) . . . but not by the highly qualified surgeon as we wished, Eileen. It was a price we couldn't afford.

BLAKE AS EILEEN. Whose hands done the deed so, Denis?

DINNY. The hands and the deed were mine, Eileen. Though to be honest I can't remember much about it. It wouldn't be every day that a son is called upon to stitch up his dead mother's pulverised face, so I had a few drinks to lessen the shock. The only previous stitching experience I had was a scarf I knitted when I was a schoolboy.

BLAKE AS EILEEN. Is that what accounts for the length of her chin?

DINNY. It is.

BLAKE AS EILEEN. And the little bobbles at the end?

DINNY. I was getting carried away at that point.

DINNY *looks at the bottle.*

Genius! Fucking genius, boy!

DINNY *runs from the bedroom and into the sitting room. He grabs the acting trophy from its shelf and kisses it.*

Is there anyone better?! Might I ever be challenged, tell me!?

SEAN AS PADDY *appears, thundering out of the wardrobe. His performance seemingly back on track.*

SEAN AS PADDY. It's Mrs Cotter's house!?! Say it isn't so, Dinny. Say it isn't so! Lying to me like that. You of the red wine and green Pringles!

DINNY. Ah bollix!

SEAN AS PADDY. That Mr Cotter told me whose house it is before he legged it into that garden shed. You know of the poverty . . .

DINNY. ' . . . before he legged it into that garden shed and into that yellow frock.' Fuck it, Sean, come on, COME ON,

BOY! Mr Cotter, yellow frock, poison in the bucket, making the blue sauce for the cooked chicken! Details, details!

SEAN. I remember, Dad!

DINNY. Remember nothing! Say the line!

SEAN AS PADDY. That Mr Cotter told me whose house it is before he legged it into that garden shed and into that yellow frock! You know of the terrible poverty me and Vera are under. You whisk us up here with your airs and graces, spin out Mammy's will and fob me off with a monthly allowance and three cans of Harp. Shame on you! Shame on you, Dinny!

When DINNY *turns away,* SEAN *grabs* HAYLEY*'s bag from off the floor and hides it behind his back.*

DINNY. He's losing it big time, Eileen.

SEAN AS PADDY. Losing nothing. Gaining is what I'm doing. Gaining my rightful half to Mammy's estate.

BLAKE AS VERA. You using a time of grief to rob a man of his rightful inheritance!

SEAN AS PADDY. Go on, Vera! Go on!!

BLAKE AS VERA. Any man with average intelligence would have copped onto you a long time ago, Dinny. But you taking advantage of Paddy's tiny minuscule brain. A man who thought that cats laid eggs. That Walt Disney discovered America . . .

SEAN AS PADDY. All right, Vera . . .

BLAKE AS VERA. . . . and that fish actually had fingers. Well, shame on you for this, Dinny!

DINNY (*snaps*). Yerrah, shut up out of that with your 'shame'!

DINNY *crashes into the kitchen as does* BLAKE, *who's now playing* MAUREEN.

HAYLEY*'s startled.*

Fuck it, Maureen we're fucked!

BLAKE AS MAUREEN. What, love?

DINNY. Paddy and Vera knows whose house it is, pet. Time to pack up Mammy and get the hell out of here.

BLAKE AS MAUREEN. Smashed are we?

DINNY. Dead in the water, love. Might get a few bob for Mammy's coffin, otherwise we're smashed.

BLAKE AS MAUREEN. Take a look in there and see if it doesn't cheer you up.

DINNY *looks and holds up some Monopoly money.*

DINNY. Holy be jaynee! What's this!?

BLAKE AS MAUREEN. Only them two other men know of it. It's half Mrs Cotter's but she doesn't have a clue, Dinny. If there was any way we could swindle the money out of her.

DINNY. Swindle this money out of Mrs Cotter, but how??!

DINNY *and* BLAKE *walk fast out of the kitchen and through the sitting room.*

A word in your ear, Eileen.

SEAN *throws the bag in to* HAYLEY.

BLAKE AS EILEEN. Why's it you told your brother Paddy that this was your house, Denis?

In her hand, HAYLEY*'s mobile phone suddenly plays the Crazy Frog version of Destiny Child's 'I'm a Survivor'.*

HAYLEY. Shit shit!

DINNY. What the fuck is that?!

SEAN *grabs* EILEEN*'s wig off* BLAKE *and continues speaking so as to mask the phone noise.*

SEAN AS EILEEN. Why's it you told your brother Paddy this was your house, Denis?

DINNY (*distracted*). 'Cause it's a deep bond between me and you, Eileen. For bonded through grief and tragedy we are.

DINNY *looking for the source of the noise.*

SEAN AS EILEEN. Tragedy, Denis? *Cein fath?*

BLAKE *is confused as he takes the wig back from* SEAN.

DINNY. That horse which killed your dear daddy as he sped through that field in his speedboat . . . that very same horse crushed my mammy as she picked gooseberries on a quiet country road.

The ring tone stops.

BLAKE AS EILEEN. The very same horse that my Dad ploughed into?

DINNY. That's the one.

BLAKE AS EILEEN. She was killed by my father so?

DINNY. And here we are left picking up the pieces, Eileen.

SEAN AS EILEEN. For her to be slain by my own father. If there was any way I could financially compensate you for this great tragedy. Anything . . . Anything at all . . .

BLAKE *suddenly realises something is up.*

HAYLEY *hides beneath the kitchen table.*

HAYLEY (*talking into the phone*). Mum, it's me! I'm in a flat on the Walworth Road . . . Will you stop talking and listen to me!

BLAKE *grabs* HAYLEY *from beneath the table. She screams and drops the phone.*

DINNY *is furious that the Farce has broken down once again.*

DINNY (*shouts*). Ah for fuck's sake!

BLAKE *drags* HAYLEY *screaming across the sitting room, picks up her coat and gets her inside the bedroom.*

DINNY *holds* SEAN *back as he tries to stop* BLAKE. *He fires him against the wardrobe.*

SEAN *collapses on the ground.*

DINNY *enters the kitchen and sees the phone on the ground.*

BLAKE *has thrown* HAYLEY *on the bed and is tying her arms behind her back. He then begins to gag her to stop her screaming.*

DINNY *picks up the phone and is amazed by it. He listens to the frantic voice on the other end.*

Hello? Am I holding a phone?

He opens the oven door and throws the phone inside and slams the door shut.

He takes the large kitchen knife from the table and leaves the kitchen. He grabs SEAN *by the hair and drags him to the armchair, making him sit.*

Standing behind him he holds the knife hard against SEAN*'s throat.*

BLAKE *steps back from* HAYLEY *who lies face down on the bed, her arms bound. He then puts on her coat.*

SEAN. I won't go on.

DINNY. Of course you will.

SEAN. I can't, Dad.

DINNY. Sean . . .

SEAN. Dad, please, I can't do it anymore.

DINNY *presses the knife in harder into* SEAN*'s throat.*

BLAKE *goes to the bedroom door and looks into the sitting room at the two of them.*

DINNY. Mammy making the macaroni cheese on a Tuesday, Sean. The two washed boys wrapped up in their dressing gowns on Saturday nights. Sunday morning and the four of us watching the Walton family on the telly with our dinner cooking in the kitchen. Friday night and in the pub for a feed of pints but I'm back home to kiss you little boys to beddy-byes just like Daddy Walton would. (*Slight pause.*) The family routine keeping things safe, Sean. I lived like that in Cork. I was a good man. (*A long pause.*) You looking in at Paddy and Vera dead on the floor like you said. My hand shaking. Real blood on the carpet. Me telling your mam, 'I'm off to London to make my fortune, Maureen. I'll send for you, Maureen, and we will be happy.' Her little kiss to me and telling me, 'Leave now.' I'm about to leave but I see you looking at me. Looking for answers, aren't ya? I turn and go. I go. In London and I'm standing in the roundabout in Elephant and Castle with all its noise and people, fuck it. 'Run, Dinny boy. Run.' Start running and get inside to Paddy's flat. These pictures of Paddy and Vera on the walls looking down at me, you see them? Asking me questions I can't answer, Sean. With every breath more scared of them. (*Slight pause.*) There's a knock on the door and it's you two boys standing there off the bus from Cork City, by jaynee. Sent by Mammy to ask me back to Cork, aren't ya. My little boys back to me. 'Hello little boys. Come on in, boys.' I wrap you up in a towel and hold ya. 'All right boys! Sure it's Daddy here, look. Ohh my little John Boy and Jim Bob! It's lovely to see ya again, boys!' To calm you down, Sean, I start to tell you the story of me and Paddy on Robert's Cove beach. Me with Daddy's towel wrapping Paddy up and keeping him safe. For days I play that story over and over for you and Blakey and it brings us some calm and peace of mind. The telling of the story . . . it helps me, Sean. (*A pause.*) 'Daddy?' 'Yes, Seanie?' 'What happened back home in Cork, Daddy?' (*A pause.*) I start to tell a new story. (*Almost breaks.*) My head, Sean.

DINNY *clutches at his head in real pain.*

SEAN *just looks at him.*

The pain slowly goes. He lowers his hands from his head.

A pause.

DINNY *looks right through him.*

We're making a routine that keeps our family safe. Isn't that what we've done here?

A slight pause.

SEAN. But none of these words are true.

A pause.

DINNY. It's my truth, nothing else matters. (*A pause*.) You can never leave here without poor Blake, can you, Sean?

SEAN. No, Dad.

DINNY. 'No, Dad.' To step outside and just little you all alone out there in the world, imagine that?

SEAN*'s eyes fill with tears*.

It could never happen, Sean, answer me.

SEAN. I couldn't be alone outside, Dad.

DINNY. No need, Seanie boy, no need at all.

SEAN *crying a little and* DINNY *embraces him*.

A pause.

You'll never tell Blake what you seen that last day, Sean?

SEAN. I wouldn't do that to him.

DINNY. A simple boy best kept in the dark, isn't he?

SEAN. It's a better place to be.

A pause.

DINNY. To kill me would only turn you into your dad. Isn't that what you're thinking, Sean? Answer me, boy.

A long pause.

So you're not going to kill me then?

A pause.

Hah?

SEAN *doesn't answer*.

Hearing enough, BLAKE *returns to* HAYLEY *and starts to untie her*.

It would never happen on *The Waltons*. Can't imagine John Boy or Jim Bob raising a nasty hand to Daddy Walton, can ya? Never in a million years, despite all those wood-carving tools hanging about their house, would you see such a thing on Walton Mountain, Sean.

The embrace breaks and DINNY *looks at* SEAN.

Get back to my story. Get ready for the big finish, Sean.
Soon Paddy's hole will strike and off to meet the good
Lord, God bless him. Play it big and clear for me, won't ya?

SEAN. I will, Dad.

DINNY. Acting trophy could be yours, Sean. I'm rooting for
you, boy.

A pause.

SEAN. Will you let her go when we finish today?

DINNY. I will let her go if you're a good boy to me.

SEAN. All right, Dad.

HAYLEY *sits on the bed with* BLAKE *standing in her coat
looking down at her.*

HAYLEY. Do you want to be me?

BLAKE. No.

BLAKE *takes off her coat and hands it to her.*

HAYLEY. How long have you been doing this? (*Slight pause.*)
Can't you leave?

BLAKE *doesn't answer. A pause.*

BLAKE. If Sean can go, you'll be with him? You won't leave
Sean alone outside, promise me.

A slight pause.

HAYLEY. I'll stay with him.

BLAKE. Cross your heart and hope to die.

A slight pause.

HAYLEY. Cross my heart and hope to die.

A pause.

BLAKE. I can finish it so.

For the final time DINNY *plays 'A Nation Once Again' on
the tape recorder.*

BLAKE and SEAN take up their positions. BLAKE goes to the kitchen and stands looking into the coffin as EILEEN and SEAN stands where SEAN AS PADDY was standing previously.

DINNY looks at HAYLEY as she makes her way back over to the kitchen. She drops her coat by the door.

She looks towards SEAN and him at her. But she knows she's by herself now. She enters the kitchen and finishes preparing the lunch.

Everything in its proper place and DINNY turns off the tape recorder and enters the kitchen fast.

DINNY. So what exactly are you saying about compensation, Eileen, for my mother's death at the hands of your daddy's speedboat. We can go halves, is it?

BLAKE AS EILEEN. This terrific money could all be yours, Denis. Just say the word and it could be you and me . . .

BLAKE AS MAUREEN (*snaps*). Dinny!

DINNY *and* BLAKE AS EILEEN (*startled*). Ahhh!

DINNY. Yerrah for fuck sake, Maureen, do you have to creep around like that!?

BLAKE AS MAUREEN. It's the money you're after and not that slapper, right? (*Pleading.*) You wouldn't leave me for Eileen, Dinny?

DINNY (*whispering*). Course I wouldn't, sweetheart. You'll have plenty of dinner days ahead of ya. Now shut up and cook!

DINNY exits the kitchen. SEAN AS PADDY turns away from him and enters the bedroom.

SEAN AS PADDY. There he is, the man who tried to rob me blind.

BLAKE enters the stage right wardrobe.

Stay away from me now for I have no family but for Mammy here.

DINNY. She's dead, Paddy. She's dead.

SEAN AS PADDY. I'm aware she's dead, Dinny. Well aware of that fact. You've tricked me for the last time, boy! A brother of mine you are no longer.

BLAKE *re-enters as* JACK *wearing a yellow frock. He holds a bucket with a yellow poison symbol painted on it. He enters the kitchen and starts to boil up some milk in a pan, and empties some of the blue contents of the bucket into it.* HAYLEY *looks on.*

DINNY. Seeing our dead mammy on that country road it threw me into a terrible despair. Lies I started to spin. Lies against the only brother I ever had. Sure I couldn't carry on with you cut out from my life, Paddy.

SEAN AS PADDY. You have done for ten years.

DINNY. That's right, you're right. But this afternoon has set me straight, Paddy. The bond is being built, I swear it.

SEAN AS PADDY. It is?

DINNY. You're my brother, Paddy, and for the life of me I don't know why I like ya. A sad day today with our mammy stuck in that box but a happy day for our reunion. So what say you of a reconciliation, oh little brother of mine? (*He holds out a can of beer.*)

SEAN AS PADDY *grabs it and knocks it back fast.*

SEAN *exits the bedroom and meets* BLAKE *who exits the kitchen where he's left* HAYLEY *stirring the pan of milk.*

BLAKE AS VERA. Mr Cotter's in the kitchen, Peter, with a bucket of poison! A yellow frock he has on! I caught Paddy wearing a pair of my knickers once. Standing on a chair and hanging a light bulb he was. It was like watching *The Dam Busters*. Sooner or later the walls of them knickers were bound to . . .

SEAN AS PETER. You know it's difficult for me to be hearing that, Vera sweetheart.

BLAKE AS VERA. You can imagine what it was like seeing it.

SEAN AS PETER. So Jack must be planning to poison me and my sister Eileen so the money can all be his. Well, we'll see about that!

BLAKE *enters the kitchen as* JACK.

BLAKE AS JACK. Just pour it over the chicken like I said, Maureen! I'm not standing here arguing with you about savoury sauces when there's a coffin of money that needs liberating.

During the following, SEAN *lights a fire lighter and throws it into the right wardrobe.*

DINNY (*entering kitchen*). Ah Mr Cotter!

BLAKE AS JACK. Suppose you're wondering what I'm doing wearing this yellow frock?

DINNY. Looks like you're making a sauce for the chicken, Jack.

BLAKE AS JACK. True but the bigger picture will speak of my new-found freedom, Denis.

DINNY. A fight worth fighting for if you don't mind me saying so, Jackie.

DINNY *pats him on the backside.*

BLAKE AS JACK. Exactly the sort of confidence boost that's needed before facing the dragon-lady herself!

BLAKE *exits the kitchen.*

Afternoon, Eileen!

BLAKE AS EILEEN (*screeches*). Oh my sweet Jesus!

Suddenly BLAKE *covers* SEAN*'s mouth with his hand.*

BLAKE. I'm ready to kill her if that's what it takes.

SEAN, *freaked, slaps his hand away.*

SEAN. No, Blake!

BLAKE. Just like Dad, Sean!

DINNY (*to* HAYLEY). What the hell's he up to, Maureen?

Slight pause.

HAYLEY. What?

BLAKE *and* SEAN *freeze and look through the open kitchen door.*

DINNY (*smiling*). So you got the lunch made the way I told ya, Maureen?

HAYLEY. Yeah.

DINNY. 'Yes, Dinny.'

HAYLEY. Yes, Dinny.

DINNY. Good girl. Little pink wafers too?

HAYLEY. I broke them up and made them into a heart shape like you said.

He smiles back to BLAKE *and* SEAN.

DINNY. Good work, Maureen. And what's that weird smell, love?

HAYLEY. Just coloured milk, I think.

DINNY *takes* MAUREEN*'s wig off* BLAKE*'s head and puts it on* HAYLEY.

BLAKE *gets the kitchen knife from the coffee table.* SEAN *tries to wrestle it off him.*

DINNY. What's that weird smell, love? (*Instructing* HAYLEY *in her line.*) 'You've got to stay away from the chicken, Dinny.'

HAYLEY (*crying, slowly*). You've got to stay away from the chicken, Dinny.

DINNY. Oh Jesus, love, I can't. Sure amn't I famished for chicken. A day of deceit and lies and I'm fit to eat a horse, by jaynee. (*Instructing her.*) 'Mr Cotter's trying to poison his wife and Peter with the chicken.'

BLAKE *walks fast into the wardrobe.*

SEAN *relieved that he's gone but still freaked out.*

HAYLEY. Mr Cotter's trying to poison his wife and Peter with the chicken.

DINNY. Poison, Maureen?

HAYLEY (*offering a new line*). Well, I saw Mr Cotter with a bucket of poison. He got me to mix it with the milk to pour it over the chicken.

DINNY (*impressed*). So he wants you to put the poisoned sauce on the chicken to kill Peter and Eileen and trick them by saying that it is in fact your special sauce, Maureen?

HAYLEY. I suppose.

DINNY (*explaining*). See, that way Peter and Vera will take the poisoned chicken thinking that it's just one of Maureen's savoury sensations. Do your new line again.

HAYLEY. I saw Mr Cotter with a bucket of poison. He got me to mix it with the milk to pour it over the chicken.

DINNY. Well, far be it for me to stand in his way. Pour away, Maureen!

DINNY *makes* HAYLEY *pour the sky-blue sauce over the pieces of chicken.* DINNY *gives* SEAN *the 'thumbs up'.*

(*To* HAYLEY.) Fair dues. You're keeping up so far.

BLAKE *is heard screaming from the smoking wardrobe.*

By jaynee what's this?!

DINNY *races into the sitting room.*

BLAKE, *as his seven-year-old self, appears out of the wardrobe carrying a smouldering stuffed dog with a tent pole up its backside.* SEAN *quickly joins him.*

Speak up and don't be hiding nothing from your daddy.

BLAKE. Minding our own business we were.

SEAN. Big barks and Bouncer hops over the fence like a wild horse.

BLAKE. Wild he is from the pain of the tent pole still up his arse, Dad.

SEAN. It didn't seem right that one of God's animals could be in such torture so Blake made chase.

BLAKE. He took some chasing though. Through the estate and back again.

SEAN. Cornered back in the garden with the pole like a deadly weapon in Bouncer's backside. Into the garden shed he runs. We follow him inside the shed, Dad, and there he lies almost dead, the poor thing.

BLAKE. Pull with all my might and that pole wouldn't budge an inch.

SEAN. Lubrication it needed. Some figure of liquid in a bottle on a shelf I applied to the doggy.

BLAKE. Still not a budge no matter how hard I pulled.

SEAN. He's frozen with the soaking now and Blake tells me to stick his shaking battered body next to the two-bar heater. When BANG!!

BLAKE. He's lit up like a firework all of a sudden! Sure when did Sean ever see methylated spirits, Dad?

SEAN. And when did I hear such screaming from one animal. Flames firing him back on his feet and Bouncer's away like a bat out of hell.

BLAKE. Thankfully the sorry sight came to a stop shortly afterwards.

DINNY. Heart attack, was it?

SEAN. Blake struck him clean with the shovel, Dad.

BLAKE. In fairness he took a few strikes. He was a great little fighter.

DINNY. Good lads.

BLAKE and SEAN exit with the smouldering stuffed dog through the right wardrobe.

A pause.

(*To* HAYLEY.) You didn't see that coming.

HAYLEY. No.

DINNY. Tying up loose ends, teasing out the big finish.
(*Shouting.*) Move it, lads! Move it!

SEAN *and* BLAKE *re-enter immediately.* BLAKE *still
holds the kitchen knife in his hand and* SEAN *sees this.*

SEAN. Fuck it, he's allowing her to leave, Blake! We can get
back to normal! Tell him, Dad!

DINNY (*announcing big*). Maureen, the chicken, love.

SEAN *tries to take the knife off* BLAKE.

SEAN. Please, Blake, no!!

DINNY (*shouts*). Maureen, move it!

HAYLEY *enters still wearing* MAUREEN*'s wig and
carrying the chicken on a tray.*

She looks at SEAN *but he looks helpless.*

Hang on a sec!

DINNY *takes his moisturiser and whitens* HAYLEY*'s face.*

That's more like it. Lovely, Maureen! (*Snaps.*) Kitchen,
Sean! Sean as Peter, come on, come on! Poison the lager,
sneaky Pete, give it to Jack, do it, do it!

SEAN AS PETER *goes to the kitchen and sees the bucket
of 'poison'. He empties some of its contents into a can of
beer. He leans over against the sideboard and holds his
head momentarily.*

You like the look of your Mammy, Blake.

BLAKE. Yes, Dad. (*Slight pause.*) Scream!

BLAKE *suddenly does a movement where he turns quickly
towards the wardrobe and holds his arms above his head.
He drops his arms and turns back to the kitchen entrance.*

Scream!

*Again he does the movement. Again he turns back. He's
practising something.*

Scream!

Again the movement. DINNY *looks on bemused.*

DINNY. Feck it, you're some tulip. (*With energy.*) Chicken everyone?!

BLAKE *takes the tray from* HAYLEY *and indicates for her to return to the kitchen.*

SEAN (*snaps*). Fuck it!

SEAN *quickly opens up a drawer in the kitchen and takes out a knife. He faces the kitchen entrance. He then puts the knife in the pocket of his jacket.*

SEAN AS PETER *appears through the other door, holding the can of 'poisoned' lager as* HAYLEY *enters the kitchen.*

BLAKE AS JACK *snatches the can of beer off* SEAN AS PETER.

BLAKE AS JACK. Cheers, Peter.

SEAN AS PETER. Be my guest.

BLAKE AS VERA (*whispering*). Is that lager poisoned then, Peter?

SEAN AS PETER. The scene's set and soon on a beach we'll lie, Vera.

BLAKE AS JACK. Chicken, Dinny?

DINNY. No chicken for me, Jackie, today's grief has tied my stomach into a tight knot smaller than a gnat's arse.

SEAN AS PADDY. Nor me, Jack. My stomach couldn't handle solids. 'Less you can liquidise that chicken into a savoury shake, it's useless to me.

BLAKE AS JACK. Some of Maureen's special sauce then, Paddy?

SEAN AS PADDY (*eyeing up his can of beer*). There's only one sauce you're holding that interests me.

BLAKE AS JACK *holds the beer out to* SEAN AS PADDY *but, as is his physical catchphrase, pulls it away at the last moment and knocks it back fast.*

Sacriligious, boy. Sacriligious.

BLAKE AS JACK. And finally you Eileen, my wife. A little bit of food needed after the shock of seeing your husband looking so good in a frock?

BLAKE AS EILEEN. It's a whole chicken that's needed, Jack.

BLAKE AS EILEEN *wolfs down a half of chicken.*

BLAKE AS JACK. Eat away, Eileen! Eat away!

BLAKE AS JACK *laughs but suddenly a jolt of pain in his stomach as the poison kicks in. He stares at the can he just drank from.*

(*Groaning.*) I'll be feeling this in the morning.

BLAKE AS JACK *collapses and dies.*

SEAN AS PETER. Let's eat to our bright future so, Vera.

BLAKE AS VERA *is up fast.*

BLAKE AS VERA. Jack dead, then?

SEAN AS PETER. Never again to don the nylons, Vera.

BLAKE AS VERA. Feed us a leg off that chicken so and let us toast our new-found love, Peter!

A chicken leg each and they feed each other.

SEAN AS PADDY (*shocked*). What's this, Vera!?

Suddenly he holds his heart in pain.

Oh good God no. Not now! Not here!

DINNY. Paddy? Paddy, what is it, little brother?!

SEAN AS PADDY. The wife's turned, Dinny. Turned from me with that knobber Peter and in doing so has fired my fragile hole.

SEAN AS PADDY *drops to his knees.*

It's smaller I'm getting! Smaller!

DINNY. You're on your knees, Paddy.

SEAN AS PADDY. So I am! But sure isn't every Irishman! (*Screams.*) ERIN GO BRAGH!

SEAN AS PADDY *falls over on the floor and dies.*

BLAKE AS VERA. With Paddy the husband gone I'm all yours, Peter love!

BLAKE AS VERA *holds his stomach in pain.*

Oh sweet Jesus! What poisoned trickery is this?

SEAN AS PETER (*holding his stomach in pain*). I fear we've come undone, Vera. Our budding love affair cut short and a shame I'll never get to see you in the nip!

BLAKE AS VERA. Likewise, Peter! It would have been nice to wake up to a virile man as opposed to my Paddy who God bless him was hung like a hamster.

They both drop to their knees and hold hands.

They collapse dead.

BLAKE *gets up and puts on* EILEEN*'s wig.*

DINNY *looks at* BLAKE AS EILEEN.

DINNY. Eileen, love, don't tell me you had a piece of that poisoned chicken, did ya?

BLAKE AS EILEEN. Never a woman to pass up free grub, Dinny. And never a better man has profited from death. (*Holding his stomach and dropping to his knees.*) The money is all yours! Oh the pain, Dinny, the pain. For me to be cut down in my prime. A woman to be robbed of what the world has to offer! Like a banker without a bank, a journalist without a journal, a painter without paint . . .

DINNY. All right, Blake!

BLAKE AS EILEEN. Cheerio, oh chosen one.

BLAKE AS EILEEN *dies.*

A pause.

DINNY *rushes into the kitchen all excited and starts filling his pockets with Monopoly money.*

SEAN *and* BLAKE *get to their feet and stand opposite each other as they hold their knives in their hands.*

The two brothers stare at each other as DINNY *continues inside the kitchen.*

BLAKE. I'm ready to kill her.

SEAN. I won't let you do it, Blake.

BLAKE. A coward like you?!

DINNY (*shouts inside*). Wardrobe, Sean! Move it! SEAN!

BLAKE *grabs* SEAN *and throws him into the wardrobe. He puts a large latch on it to lock* SEAN *inside.*

SEAN (*from inside*). NO!

DINNY (*triumphant*). Well, Maureen, the day of the dead it most certainly is! But even in violent death some glimmer of hope must be sought. Sure aren't people great all the same. A kick in the face and they'll come up smiling. Backs to the wall and it's best foot forward.

DINNY *leaves the kitchen for the sitting room.* HAYLEY *stands at the kitchen door looking at him.*

So away to London I am. Away to treble my new-found wealth and build for us a castle to overlook the English scum. There we'll sit, Maureen, lording over the lot of them, a bit of Cork up there in the sky. It's soon I'll call for you, Maureen. (*Rubbing moisturiser into his face.*) 'Tween now and then keep youthful, love, and I too won't change a jot. Lines won't grow on this face and hair still as thick as a brush, by Christ.

BLAKE AS MAUREEN (*firm*). Yes, Dinny. I'll wait home in Cork for you.

DINNY *throws an arm around* BLAKE *and gives him a little hug. The knife held tight in* BLAKE*'s hand about to strike.*

DINNY. A day of twists and turns and ducks and dives and terrible shocks. A story to be retold, no doubt, and cast in lore. For what are we, Maureen, if we're not our stories?

BLAKE. We're the lost and the lonely.

DINNY. Away to London! Gather around, my little boys!

Come and kiss your daddy a final farewell!

BLAKE *fires the knife into* DINNY*'s back.*

DINNY *gasps.* BLAKE *pulls out the knife, turns* DINNY *towards him quickly and stabs him in the stomach hard.*

(In pain he continues.) Away . . . away . . .

BLAKE *(quietly he prompts him).* 'Away but soon . . .'

DINNY. Away but soon . . . Trophy, Blake. Trophy.

BLAKE *hands him his acting trophy.*

BLAKE. 'Away but soon and I'll return to Cork, Maureen.' Say it, Dad.

DINNY *watches the blood pour from his stomach.*

DINNY. Fuck it, that's some acting. Real blood. The blood and bandage, Blake, hah? *(Slight pause.)* Away but soon and I'll return to Cork, Maureen.

DINNY *kisses his trophy.*

HAYLEY *stands in the kitchen entrance petrified.*

BLAKE *(to* HAYLEY*).* Latch.

HAYLEY *goes to the wardrobe and holds the latch. She looks at* BLAKE.

(Calmly to HAYLEY*.)* Scream.

HAYLEY *screams and opens the latch fast.*

BLAKE *suddenly does the movement where he turns quickly towards the wardrobe and holds his arms above his head.*

SEAN *runs from the wardrobe and drives his knife into* BLAKE*'s stomach.*

DINNY *slumps to the ground dead.*

BLAKE *slumps against* SEAN.

Only now does SEAN *see his father dead, sees* HAYLEY *alive and realises what his brother has done.*

He takes the knife out of BLAKE*'s stomach. Blood pours onto the floor.*

BLAKE, *close to death, kisses* SEAN *gently on the lips.*

BLAKE. Now leave, love.

BLAKE *dies.*

Terrified, HAYLEY *runs to the front door, scrambles to open the last lock, opens it and exits fast leaving the door open.*

SEAN *lowers* BLAKE *to the floor. He places the knife down on the coffee table. His hand shaking, he takes a drink from a can of beer. He then looks towards the open front door.*

Reaching under the armchair he takes up the biscuit tin and opens it. He looks inside and takes out a handful of cash. He stands and puts the cash in his pocket.

He looks at the tape recorder in front of him. He rewinds the tape. He presses the tape recorder and 'An Irish Lullaby' begins to play.

He walks to the front door and stops just inside the flat.

He stands there for some time looking out.

He then closes the door and begins to lock it.

He faces back into the flat.

Now quickly and with purpose. SEAN *resets the coffins, lager, chicken.*

We watch him quickly move through the main events of the first act. DINNY *and* PADDY*'s entrance,* VERA *and* MAUREEN*'s entrance, the cheese and crackers on the plate, himself being struck by the frying pan,* JACK *and* PETER*'s entrance,* DINNY *fainting, and finally the Monopoly money being thrown into the air. This all lasts two minutes.*

SEAN *fires a look towards the front door.*

He walks out to the sitting room.

He picks up HAYLEY*'s coat and puts it on, he lifts up her bag and places it on his shoulder. He takes a plastic Tesco bag from the ground and holds it.*

He turns his back to us as he stands at the door. He's applying something to his face.

'An Irish Lullaby' comes to an end.

Silence.

SEAN *turns. He's covered his face in* DINNY*'s brown shoe polish. He's making* HAYLEY*'s entrance.*

Loud guttural rhythmic music fades up and fills the stage and auditorium.

The light eventually fades down on SEAN *as we watch him calmly lose himself in a new story.*

Blackout.

Silence.

Curtain falls.

The End.

A Nick Hern Book

The Walworth Farce first published in Great Britain in 2007 as a
paperback original by Nick Hern Books Limited, 14 Larden Road,
London W3 7ST, in association with Druid Theatre Company

Cover image: © John Foley at Bite! Associates, www.bitedesign.com
Cover design: Ned Hoste, 2H

Typeset by Nick Hern Books, London
Printed and bound in Great Britain by CPI Bookmarque, Croydon,
Surrey

A CIP catalogue record for this book is available from the British
Library

ISBN 978 1 85459 997 1